INDY COFFEE GUIDE
WALES NO I
IS SUPPORTED BY

## CAKESMITHS
CAKES FOR COFFEE SHOPS

## DAISY BANK DAIRY

salt

# Zettle
*by PayPal*

# FOR BREW FREAKS, BEAN GEEKS

# AND THE SIMPLY CURIOUS ...

**Indy Coffee Guide team:**

Richard Bailey, Nick Cooper,
Charlotte Cummins, Kathryn Lewis,
Abi Manning, Melissa Morris, Kirstie Newton,
Tamsin Powell, Jo Rees, Rosanna Rothery,
Ben Sibley, Melissa Stewart, Mark Tibbles
and Selena Young.

A big thank you to the Indy Coffee Guide
committee (meet them on page 112) for their
expertise and enthusiasm, and to our sponsors
Cakesmiths, Daisy Bank Dairy and Zettle.

Coffee shops, cafes and roasteries are invited
to be included in the guide based on meeting
criteria set by the committee, which includes
the use of speciality beans, providing a
high-quality coffee experience for visitors
and being independently run.

For information on Indy Coffee Guides for
England: North, Midlands and East; England:
The South; Ireland; and Scotland, visit:

# INDYCOFFEE.GUIDE
indycoffeeguide

The right of Salt Media to be identified as the author
of this work has been asserted by it in accordance with
the Copyright, Designs and Patents Act 1988.

A catalogue record of the book is available from the
British Library.

© Salt Media Ltd
Published by Salt Media Ltd 2023
ISBN 9781739166830
saltmedia.co.uk
01271 859299
ideas@saltmedia.co.uk

3/3.20

2.80/3

40/3·40

COFFEE

# CONTENTS

**Page**

# WELCOME

It's my absolute pleasure to welcome you to the first edition of *Indy Coffee Guide Wales*. As a resident of Cardiff for over a decade, I've watched Wales' speciality coffee scene blossom and am thrilled it's grown large enough to warrant a guide all of its own.

When we first covered South Wales in our South-West England and South Wales guide in 2016, we included just ten Welsh coffee shops and three roasteries. This edition features 50 handpicked coffee shops, ten roasteries and a barista trainer in Wales – testament to the country's thriving coffee community.

Leaf through the guide and, from Cardiff to Carmarthen and Llandudno to Llandeilo, you'll find outstanding indie businesses serving top-notch coffee. These are the kind of places where you can natter with the owner as they prepare your flat white, pop into a roastery shop to pick up beans fresh from the drum, or tuck into hot-from-the-oven pastries served by the artisans who crafted them.

Every inclusion in this book offers a one-of-a-kind experience – the exact opposite of those chains reproducing identikit venues around the world. We're confident you'll love each and every one of the coffee shops, cafes and roasteries in these pages, and can't wait to hear about your coffee trips across Wales. Don't forget to share your highlights with us on Instagram.

Enjoy!

**Kathryn Lewis**
Editor
Indy Coffee Guides
🅞 *indycoffeeguide*

# HOW TO USE THE GUIDE

# CAFES

Coffee shops and cafes where you can drink top-notch speciality coffee. We've split the guide into areas to help you find places near you.

# ROASTERIES

Meet the leading speciality coffee roasters and discover where to source beans. Find them after the cafes in each area.

Facilities available at the venues are shown via symbols at the bottom of each page, including if Welsh (Cymraeg) is spoken.

# MAPS

Every cafe and roastery has a number so you can find them either on the area map at the start of each section or on the detailed city maps. Areas are defined by the Senedd constituencies.

# MORE GOOD STUFF

Discover **more good coffee shops** and **more good roasteries** at the back of the book.

Follow us on Instagram
🄾 indycoffeeguide

# YOUR ADVENTURES START HERE

57 THE ANGEL BAKERY

# DAISY BANK DAIRY

# Proud dairy sponsors of the Indy Coffee Guide

Like our supporters throughout the coffee industry, we're passionate about everything we do.

Barista milk specialist ✔
Single origin ✔
Organic and ethical ✔
Grass fed ✔
Non-homognised ✔
Plastic free and reduced plastic options ✔
Freindly and reliable service throughout ✔
Wales and beyond ✔
Delicious ✔

Hit us up on our socials if you'd like to discuss how you can become a new supporter of ours.

#teamdaisybankdairy

DRINKS ME

ESPRESSO        2.65    FILT
MACCHIATO       2.70    ICEL
FLAT WHITE      3.10    HOT
LONG BLACK      2.80    CHA
CAPPUCCINO      3.20    TEA
LATTE           3.30    MO
AMERICANO       2.95

SYRUPS
EXTRA SH
ALT MILK

SANREMO

Guest
Filter

ORIGIN: PERU,
          SOUTH AMERICA
PROCESS: WASHED,
          SUN DRIED
TASTE NOTE: •creamy body
            •soft citrus acidity
            •milk choc, nutty

**7** PROVIDERO COFFEE HOUSE – LLANDUDNO

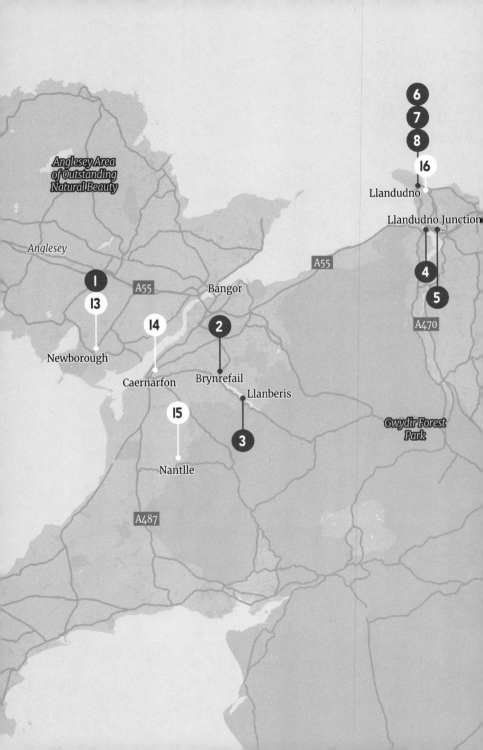

Anglesey Area
of Outstanding
Natural Beauty

Anglesey

Newborough

A55

Bangor

Caernarfon

Brynrefail

Llanberis

Nantlle

A487

A55

Llandudno

Llandudno Junction

A470

Gwydir Forest
Park

1
13
14
2
15
3
6
7
8
16
4
5

**17**

**9**
Prestatyn

A55

A55

## ● CAFES

1 Dragon Roastery Coffee Bar
2 Caban Cafe
3 Frân Las
4 The Jester's Tower
5 Providero Coffee House – Llandudno Junction
6 Dudley and George's
7 Providero Coffee House – Llandudno
8 Botanical Babe Plants
9 Caffeina
10 Tabernacl
11 Bank Street Social
12 Riverbanc

**10**
**11**
Wrexham

**12**
Llangollen

## ○ ROASTERIES

13 Dragon Roastery
14 Coffi Dre
15 Poblado Coffi
16 Heartland Coffee Roasters
17 Mug Run Coffee

A483

Find more good cafes and roasteries on pages 108–111

*All locations are approximate*

# 1 DRAGON ROASTERY COFFEE BAR

Stryd Pendref, Newborough, Anglesey, LL61 6TB

dragonroastery.co.uk | 07949 393168

**f** *dragonroastery* 📷 *dragonroastery*

If you spot this cherry-red roaming coffee bar on your travels around Anglesey and North Wales, halt what you're doing and make a pit stop.

Dragon Roastery's horsebox-turned-cafe is no ordinary mobile set-up. The high-spec, solar-powered conversion dishes out a huge selection of own-roasted beans in a variety of serve styles from a tiny space no bigger than, well, a horsebox. There's even room on board for mixology kit and artisan spirits for its evening alter ego as a cocktail bar.

## TIP BUY BEANS TO BREW AT HOME FROM THE HORSEBOX

It's available to hire for all manner of occasions, from festivals and private parties to weddings and corporate events, and includes two baristas/bartenders and travel to the event.

All the coffees are roasted at the Dragon Roastery on Anglesey, including the popular Espresso blend which scooped a Great Taste award for its unique mix of five coffees. Try it as a flat white, or opt for one of the single-origin options as batch filter or V60 pourover.

**Established**
2018

**Key roaster**
Dragon Roastery

**Brewing method**
Espresso, V60, batch filter

**Machine**
Rancilio Classe 6

**Grinder**
Mazzer Super Jolly

**Opening hours**
As per event

ANGLESEY

**REUSABLES ACCEPTED**

**BIKE FRIENDLY**

**DOGS WELCOME**

**BUY BEANS IN STORE**

**COFFEE COURSES**

**OUTDOOR SEATING**

**CYMRAEG**

24

# 2 CABAN CAFE

Yr Hen Ysgol, Brynrefail, Caernarfon, Gwynedd, LL55 3NR
caban-cyf.org | 01286 685500

**f** *caban.brynrefail* **@** *cafficaban*

One of Wales' longest running social enterprises, Caban has been at the heart of its community for two decades.

The unique semi-circular, glass-encased space has serious treehouse vibes. When the weather allows, sit on the decking among the foliage to bask in nature while savouring a cup of Caban's exclusive blend, made in collaboration with local roastery Poblado. The mix of Guatemalan, Ugandan and Sumatran beans is the trusty house espresso and the perfect base for a fantastic flat white.

## TIP THIS IS A GREAT SPOT FOR KICKING BACK WITH A COFFEE WHILE YOUR EV CHARGES

A guest grinder hosts beans from fellow North Wales roastery Heartland, and there's usually a single origin available as V60 too. Any beans on the coffee menu are also available to take home and can be ground to your specific set-up.

Located a stone's throw from the shores of Llyn Padarn and Eryri National Park, this is a popular place for the whole family to refuel after a morning of adventures. The daily specials board showcases seasonal produce in dishes such as aubergine, ricotta and mozzarella gratin.

**Established**
2003

**Key roaster**
Poblado Coffi

**Brewing method**
Espresso, V60,
batch filter

**Machine**
Victoria Arduino
Black Eagle
Gravitech

**Grinder**
Victoria Arduino
Mythos 2,
Mahlkonig EK43

**Opening hours**
Mon-Sun
9am-4pm

| WIFI | BIKE FRIENDLY | BUY BEANS IN STORE | OUTDOOR SEATING | CYMRAEG |

CAERNARFON

25

# 3 FRÂN LAS

48 Stryd Fawr, Llanberis, Caernarfon, Gwynedd, LL55 4EU

franlas.coffee

[image] franlas.coffee

**S**urrounded by views as picturesque as any in the UK, this contemporary spot on the northwestern edge of Eryri National Park is a favourite of Llanberis locals, holidaymakers, hikers and cyclists alike.

Frân Las founder Jordan Phoenix (who grew up two doors down from the premises) has made a reputation for crafting some of the largest bakes in Wales. The oversized cinnamon swirls may just about fit on your plate, but the monumental stuffed bagels and sandwiches definitely won't – those with small appetites should pack a Tupperware for leftovers.

## TIP VEGANS REJOICE! EVERYTHING, FROM CINNAMON SWIRLS TO SAUSAGE ROLLS, IS PLANT-BASED

The house hopper is packed with Hard Lines' House Party roast, a natural single-origin from Brazil delivering notes of chocolate and dried fruit. There's more from the Cardiff roastery on the rotating batch-filter menu; order yours served over ice if the weather calls for cooling down.

Before you leave, check out the selection of brewing equipment and accessories for sale, or pick up one of Frân Las' famed branded T-shirts.

**Established**
2021

**Key roaster**
Hard Lines

**Brewing method**
Espresso,
batch filter,
pourover

**Machine**
Sanremo

**Grinder**
Mahlkonig EK43,
Mahlkonig K30

**Opening hours**
Fri-Tue
9.30am–3pm

REUSABLES
ACCEPTED

DOGS
WELCOME

BUY BEANS
IN STORE

OUTDOOR
SEATING

CYMRAEG

26

# 4 THE JESTER'S TOWER

Castle Square, Castle Street, Conwy, LL32 8AY

thejesterstower.com | 01492 581450

**f** *thejesterstower* @ *thejesterstower*

This cafe within a 700-year-old tower must be one of the most unique places in the UK to savour a cup of coffee. Where else can you order a flat white, meet an official jester (owner Erwyd le Fol currently holds the title for Conwy) and then visit a 900-year-old mummified mermaid on the way to the loo?

Located in the town's medieval quarter, The Jester's Tower attracts both serious coffee fans and those who are fascinated by curios and oddities. The cafe shares a building with The Unseen Repository (North Wales' only permanent museum of strange things), so visiting one almost always results in a trip to the other.

## TIP OPENING HOURS CHANGE SEASONALLY, SO CHECK THE WEBSITE BEFORE YOU VISIT

Local roastery Heartland stocks the cafe's grinder with its Landmark blend, a Great Taste award-winner delivering notes of chocolate and nut. The Swiss Water Process decaf and occasional guest options (house faves include an Ethiopian Yirgacheffe and Colombia Sweet Valley) are also roasted by the team at Heartland.

Stick around to enjoy your pick of the coffee offering and food menu with views of the ancient quayside.

**Established**
2021

**Key roaster**
Heartland Coffee Roasters

**Brewing method**
Espresso, V60, AeroPress, batch filter

**Machine**
Sanremo Zoe Vision

**Grinder**
Anfim Pratica

**Opening hours**
Mon-Tue, Thu-Fri
10am-3pm
Sat
9.30am-5pm
Sun
9.30am-4pm
(seasonal opening hours)

**REUSABLES ACCEPTED**

**WIFI**

**DOGS WELCOME**

**BUY BEANS IN STORE**

**OUTDOOR SEATING**

**CYMRAEG**

# 5 PROVIDERO COFFEE HOUSE - LLANDUDNO JUNCTION

148 Conway Road, Llandudno Junction, Conwy, LL31 9DU

providero.co.uk | 01492 338220

*f bigprov* *@ providerocoffee*

This tiny two-storey cafe (Little Prov, as it's affectionately known) is the OG bricks-and-mortar Providero coffee shop. It attracts a steady stream of locals and commuters travelling to and from Llandudno Junction train station, as well as those making a pit stop off the busy North Wales Expressway.

Over the past 12 months, Little Prov has enjoyed a spruce up, with new exterior branding and an interior reshuffle to make it feel lighter and more spacious. There's also a new retail section stocked with beans, brewing kit and locally produced candles.

## TIP HUNGRY? BROWSE THE MENU OF TOPPED SOURDOUGH TOASTS

Downstairs is a compact, busy space where you can have a natter with the team as they craft you a cup of the latest single origin, while upstairs is an area for quiet contemplation on the comfy corner sofa.

Llandudno's very own speciality roastery, Heartland, supplies the goods for the duo of grinders. Landmark is the house blend and a single-origin option is rotated every six weeks – the Little Prov team are guided by customer feedback and adapt the coffee offering to meet local demand.

**Established**
2014

**Key roaster**
Heartland
Coffee Roasters

**Brewing method**
Espresso,
batch filter

**Machine**
Sanremo Zoe

**Grinder**
Mahlkonig EK43,
Victoria Arduino
Mythos One
Clima Pro

**Opening hours**
Mon-Sat
8am-2pm

REUSABLES ACCEPTED | WIFI | BIKE FRIENDLY | DOGS WELCOME | BUY BEANS IN STORE | CYMRAEG

# 6 DUDLEY AND GEORGE'S

127 Mostyn Street, Llandudno, Conwy, LL30 2PE
dudleyandgeorges.co.uk | 01492 701689
**f** *dudleyandgeorges* **◎** *dudleyandgeorges*

After years working in central London, Yorkshire lad Jason Pinnick finally let himself off the lead to realise his dream of opening a lifestyle shop for dogs and their humans.

The project was an immediate success and the in-house cafe that followed soon had tongues and tails wagging across Llandudno. Two-legged visitors are treated to house roasts from Swan Song in Manchester and South Wales' Big Dog Coffee, as well as guest roasts from the likes of Colonna, Sweven and Heartland.

## TIP PLANT-BASED? CHECK OUT THE NEW VEGAN MENU

If you're enjoying something tasty from the array of homemade bakes that fill the counter each morning, it's only right to treat your furry companion too. A menu full of nutritional eats designed consciously for canines includes the likes of turkey superfood salad, and wild rice with wheatgrass and salmon.

Check out the shelves before you leave – they're stacked with coffee beans, homewares, local produce and, of course, sustenance for four-pawed friends.

**Established**
2022

**Key roaster**
Multiple roasteries

**Brewing method**
Espresso, V60,
batch filter,
syphon, cold brew

**Machine**
Sanremo Verona

**Grinder**
Mahlkonig, Eureka

**Opening hours**
Mon–Sun
8am–5.30pm

REUSABLES ACCEPTED  WIFI  BIKE FRIENDLY  DOGS WELCOME  BUY BEANS IN STORE  OUTDOOR SEATING  CYMRAEG

# 7 PROVIDERO COFFEE HOUSE - LLANDUDNO

112 Upper Mostyn Street, Llandudno, Conwy, LL30 2SW

providero.co.uk | 01492 338220

**f** *bigprov* **⊙** *providerocoffee*

It's hard to create an atmosphere that instantly puts customers at ease, but the team at Providero have pulled it off. The ethos at this Llandudno hangout is all about making customers feel part of a community, whether they're a regular or have just wandered in for the first time.

Over the past 12 months, a conscious effort has been made to build a space that inspires creativity. There's lots to keep the brain ticking, from perusing local artwork to partaking in a jazz-fuelled brunch and signing up for a gong bath or yoga class in ProvSpace (its studio next door).

## TIP JOIN THE PROV CLUB AND PICK UP A BRANDED TEE, TOTE OR BEANIE

At the heart of it all, however, is the coffee. Heartland's Landmark blend is the standard serve on espresso, but there's also a single-origin option (available as filter too) which rotates every six weeks to keep regulars on their toes. Both are also available by the bag to take home.

Hungry? The Welsh cheddar and prosciutto toastie is a firm favourite, especially when paired with a hearty bowl of homemade soup. There's also a countertop cabinet stacked with fresh cakes and bakes, including plenty of options for gluten-free and vegan visitors.

**Established**
2017

**Key roaster**
Heartland
Coffee Roasters

**Brewing method**
Espresso,
batch filter

**Machine**
Sanremo Opera

**Grinder**
Mahlkonig EK43,
Eureka Zenith 65E,
Mahlkonig E65S
GbW, Victoria
Arduino Mythos
One Clima Pro

**Opening hours**
Mon-Sun
8.30am-5pm

REUSABLES ACCEPTED   WIFI   BIKE FRIENDLY   DOGS WELCOME   BUY BEANS IN STORE   OUTDOOR SEATING   CYMRAEG

# 8 BOTANICAL BABE PLANTS

66 Mostyn Street, Llandudno, Conwy, LL30 2SB
botanicalbabeplants.com | 01492 701032
*f botanicalbabee* *◎ botanical_babee*

Pass through the trailing fronds, giant leaves and swaying palms that frame the entrance of this indie plant shop to discover an oasis of speciality coffee.

Tesni Boughen has run Botanical Babe on Llandudno's Mostyn Street since 2020, but at the start of 2023 she noticed a gap in the market for a venue serving quality coffee. Instead of opening a second site, she introduced a coffee bar to her original set-up and enlisted local business Heartland (located just five minutes down the road) to roast the beans.

## TIP PAIR YOUR COFFEE WITH A BUTTERY CROISSANT FROM BENJAMIN LEE ARTISAN BAKERY

The roastery's Landmark blend is the house espresso, while its Ethiopia Guji Hambela Natural is the single-origin option on V60. Take your pick then unwind in the calming setting while the baristas prep your drink – the rattan sofa in the window is the most coveted spot in the shop.

Tesni hosts regular events in the dynamic space, including botanical yoga sessions and terrarium workshops.

**Established**
2023

**Key roaster**
Heartland Coffee Roasters

**Brewing method**
Espresso, V60

**Machine**
Sanremo F18

**Grinder**
Mahlkonig EK43, Mahlkonig E65S

**Opening hours**
Mon–Sun
8.30am–5.30pm

**REUSABLES ACCEPTED**

**WIFI**

**DOGS WELCOME**

**BUY BEANS IN STORE**

**OUTDOOR SEATING**

# 9 CAFFEINA

28 High Street, Prestatyn, Denbighshire, LL19 9BB

caffeinacoffi.co.uk

*f caffeinacoffi* *○ caffeinacoffi*

Prestatyn's speciality coffee lovers let out squeals of joy when this female-owned coffee shop opened its doors in 2021. With its creative food and drink line-up, the venue brings slick city vibes to the small coastal town and has amassed a following of fans as a result.

The small but mighty team love Big House by NewGround in Oxfordshire and serve the caramel, cherry and milk-choc-forward coffee blend as their house espresso. Guest beans vary but have recently included the jammy Padah-Lin from Myanmar, roasted by Kent's Curve Coffee. Like a left-field drinks order? Go for an iced spirulina latte.

## TIP CHECK OUT THE GIANT BIRD OF PARADISE PLANT IN THE WINDOW

The food offering brings overseas inspiration to the seaside spot, with menu additions such as açaí bowls, bagels, NYC-style stuffed cookies and vegan sausage rolls. Scoff the inventive dishes amid the calm, minimalist interior or head to the outdoor seating area to enjoy the sea breeze while you tuck in.

**Established**
2021

**Key roaster**
NewGround

**Brewing method**
Espresso

**Machine**
Victoria Arduino
Eagle One

**Grinder**
Anfim Pratica,
Mahlkonig EK43

**Opening hours**
Tue–Sat
9am–4pm
Sun
10am–3pm

PRESTATYN

REUSABLES
ACCEPTED

WIFI

BIKE
FRIENDLY

DOGS
WELCOME

BUY BEANS
IN STORE

OUTDOOR
SEATING

# 10 TABERNACL

Hope Street Church, 1-2 Hope Street, Wrexham, LL11 1BG

hopestreet.church | 07572 619057

𝐟 *tabernaclwxm*

**W**hen this church-run cafe opened in the Burton Building in Wrexham town centre, it breathed new life into an iconic venue that had lain abandoned and crumbling for over a decade. One year later, the Tabernacl team have grown a business that encompasses a trinity of principles: being ethical and sustainable, promoting community and serving quality coffee.

These values are the lifeblood that runs through Tabernacl. In a bid to ensure every member of society has the chance to benefit from the project, profits go towards the community initiatives of Hope Street Church (including its toddler group and homeless outreach). The cafe also has a pay-it-forward scheme in place and even provided a venue for the FOCUS Wales music festival.

## TIP STAY FOR A TOASTIE, SARNIE, SOUP OR BAKE (INCLUDING THE FAMOUS BIG CHUNK COOKIES)

Blossom, one of the UK's most sustainable roasteries, supplies the house beans. Adventurous sippers can switch up their order with each visit by opting for the guest roast – from the likes of Hundred House and Coaltown – on batch or V60. Pick up beans, reusable cups and home brewing essentials in the merch section to recreate the experience at home.

**Established**
2022

**Key roaster**
Blossom Coffee Roasters

**Brewing method**
Espresso, V60, batch filter

**Machine**
La Marzocco Linea PB

**Grinder**
Mahlkonig E65S GbW, Anfim Pratica

**Opening hours**
Tue–Sun
10am–4pm

**REUSABLES ACCEPTED**

**WIFI**

**DOGS WELCOME**

**BUY BEANS IN STORE**

**OUTDOOR SEATING**

**CYMRAEG**

WREXHAM

33

# 11 BANK STREET SOCIAL

5a Bank Street, Wrexham, LL11 1AH

bankstreetsocial.co.uk

𝐟 *bankstreetsocialwxm* 𝗈 *bankstsocial*

**S**ocial by name, social by nature. The team at this community-centric coffee and beer bar love a chat, so don't be surprised if you're pulled into a shop-wide conversation on any manner of topics when you visit.

The friendly vibes originate from owners and brothers Phil and Andy Gallanders, self-professed 'unofficial guides to Wrexham', cheesy pun creators (see the blackboard outside), and coffee and beer aficionados. The chatty pair love nothing more than bringing together like-minded folk – you might even spot them at food festivals, artisan markets and the odd wedding as they've just launched an events company to spread the social vibes even further.

## TIP ORDER ONE OF THE OOZING SOURDOUGH TOASTIES

Their passion for speciality brews comes in two guises: coffee and beer. The former is the award-winning Espresso Yourself blend (a rich and chocolatey crowd-pleaser combining toffee sweetness with a complex fruity edge) from Liverpool's Neighbourhood Coffee. Craft beer buffs, meanwhile, can ogle the kaleidoscope of funky cans packing the fridges, including hop-forward brews from Polly's Brew Co in Mold and a good selection of Belgian beers.

**Established**
2017

**Key roaster**
Neighbourhood
Coffee

**Brewing method**
Espresso

**Machine**
La Marzocco
Linea PB

**Grinder**
Victoria Arduino
Mythos One,
Mahlkonig EK43

**Opening hours**
Mon–Fri
8am–3pm
Sat
9am–3pm

WREXHAM

WIFI   DOGS
WELCOME   BUY BEANS
IN STORE

# 12 RIVERBANC

9 Bridge Street, Llangollen, Denbighshire, LL20 8PF
riverbanc.co.uk | 01978 799903
𝑓 *riverbanc* ⓞ *riverbanc_llangollen*

Overnight guests and daytime visitors to this outdoor-adventure hotel and cafe in Llangollen usually leave with a camera roll full of shots of both stunning landscapes and latte art.

Located in the wilds of North Wales, Riverbanc teems with thrill-seekers who've checked into one of the seven rooms to make the most of watersports on the River Dee. However, it's also a popular spot for locals and day-trippers who swing by to sip speciality coffee and tuck into cafe fodder amid gorgeous scenery.

Rain or shine, take your order outside to the covered alpine-style decking to drink in the spellbinding vista of the river, woodlands and Llangollen Bridge (one of the Seven Wonders of Wales). Inside the cafe you'll discover a cosier setting of reclaimed-wood tables, trailing houseplants and laid-back tunes.

## TIP CHECK OUT THE CRAFT WALL FILLED WITH LOCAL ART, JEWELLERY AND ACCESSORIES

Single-origin beans from Hasbean, as well as a line-up of guest roasts, are transformed into classic and not-so-classic espresso drinks. Go off-menu and join regulars in ordering a house-special flattuccino (same size as a cappuccino but less foamy and more silky) or give the mushroom coffee a whirl.

Couple your drinks order with a breakfast or lunch dish from an all-day menu that includes the likes of the full Welsh breakfast, loaded waffles and the Neato Burrito.

**Established**
2018

**Key roaster**
Hasbean

**Brewing method**
Espresso

**Machine**
Nuova Simonelli
Aurelia II

**Grinder**
Victoria Arduino
Mythos One × 2

**Opening hours**
Mon–Sun
8am–4pm

REUSABLES ACCEPTED | WIFI | BIKE FRIENDLY | DOGS WELCOME | BUY BEANS IN STORE | OUTDOOR SEATING | CYMRAEG

NORTH
WALES
ROASTERIES

# 13 DRAGON ROASTERY

Stryd Pendref, Newborough, Anglesey, Ll61 6TB

dragonroastery.co.uk | 07949 393168

*f dragonroastery* *◎ dragonroastery*

**O**n market days in Anglesey, locals make a beeline for Dragon Roastery's cherry-red vintage horsebox for their speciality fix. As the first coffee roastery on the island, it's grown a following for its punchy, full-flavoured beans.

Head roaster Felicity Homer and team source beans from across the coffee-growing belt and roast them on a quirky 1950s Vittoria drum roaster. Their most popular blend is Great Taste award-winner Espresso, a wickedly smooth mix of five beans from coffee farms across the world, which you'll find in the hoppers of cafes in North Wales and beyond.

## 'AS THE FIRST COFFEE ROASTERY ON THE ISLAND, IT'S GROWN A FOLLOWING FOR ITS PUNCHY, FULL-FLAVOURED BEANS'

Felicity loves sniffing out new and exciting single origins to experiment with at the roastery, so online customers can choose from a rotating range. Recent highlights include the dark-roast Perla Negra from Guatemala and the medium-roast San Ramon from Nicaragua. Make a bulk order from the webshop (2kg or more) and get free delivery to your door.

**Established**
2017

**Roaster make and size**
Vittoria 15kg,
Victory 5kg

**BUY BEANS ONLINE**

**CYMRAEG**

ANGLESEY

# 14 COFFI DRE

Caernarfon, Gwynedd

coffidre.cymru | 07907 603274

*f coffidre* *⊙ coffidre*

In spring 2021, operations engineer Ceurwyn Humphreys got behind the bar of his father's new cafe to pull an espresso for the first time in ten years. As he watched the coffee drip and flow into the cup below, an idea started brewing.

By the end of that summer, Ceurwyn and his business partners Haydn and Tom had launched Coffi Dre. Roughly translating into English as 'Caernarfon coffee', this is a roastery fiercely passionate about celebrating the region's language, tradition and history.

Coffees are named after local points of interest and resident artists help bring the bags to life by creating evocative illustrations for each. Twthill, a South American blend, takes its name from a nearby triangulation point, while washed Colombian Porth yr Aur ('the golden gate') refers to the 13th-century gate on the western edge of town.

**Established**
2021

**Roaster make and size**
Pacrone 5kg

## 'AT EVENTS, CEURWYN AND HAYDN SERVE CAPPUCCINOS FROM A CONVERTED HORSEBOX'

Fans can enjoy Coffi Dre's beans at home, in cafes and at events, where Ceurwyn and Haydn serve cappuccinos from a converted horsebox. The rumour is that a first bricks-and-mortar shop is on the horizon ... cyffrous iawn!

COFFEE COURSES

BUY BEANS ONLINE

BUY BEANS IN STORE

CYMRAEG

# Tools to run your coffee shop

## Zettle
*by PayPal*

zettle.com/gb/contact-us

# 15 POBLADO COFFI

Unit 1 Y Barics, Nantlle, Caernarfon, Gwynedd, LL54 6BD

pobladocoffi.co.uk | 01286 882555

*f pobladocoffi* *☺ poblado_coffi*

If you're visiting Eryri or the beautiful North Wales coast, it's worth making a detour to this coffee roastery housed in a former quarrymen's barracks.

Every Saturday morning, founder Steffan Huws extends an open invitation to anyone who wishes to join the Poblado Plodders as they leave for a communal run around the old quarry, ending with a brew and a chat back at the roastery.

In summer, the barracks' doors stay open, and locals and visiting coffee fans gather in the courtyard for alfresco sipping and cake. While the summer weekend sessions are the most popular, Steffan and team welcome roaming coffee folk for a chat and a brew any day of the week – if the door is open, the coffee machine is on.

## 'STEFFAN IS PASSIONATE ABOUT FORGING LONG-TERM RELATIONSHIPS WITH GROWERS'

At the heart of the roastery is a 15kg Giesen which roasts Poblado's curated collection of blends and single origins. Steffan is passionate about forging long-term relationships with growers, and the lots he sources from the Americas, Africa and Asia are selected for their sustainability credentials.

Signing up for one of the variety-pack subscriptions is the best way to sample the range of different beans – sippers can get the low-down on each of the coffees via the Poblado website.

**Established**
2013

**Roaster make and size**
Giesen 15kg

CAFE ON SITE | OPEN BY INVITE | BUY BEANS ONLINE | BUY BEANS IN STORE | CYMRAEG

# 16 HEARTLAND COFFEE ROASTERS

Unit 6 Cwrt Roger Mostyn, Builder Street, Llandudno, LL30 1DS

heartland.coffee | 01492 878757

🄲 *heartland.coffee*

The Heartland roasting crew care deeply about elevating the coffee experience for those at the start and end of the speciality process: the farmers and customers.

Over the past year, the team have developed ever-closer relationships with farming partners including Migoti Coffee in Burundi, whose Murambi Hill Natural has been a standout roast. They've also found success with Café Granja La Esperanza's Colombia Sweet Valley beans. This rare gem is an experimental high-altitude coffee, fermented for 15 hours at a controlled temperature, moved to a dehumidifier for 72 hours to dry, and then milled.

## 'THE HEARTLAND ROASTING CREW CARE DEEPLY ABOUT ELEVATING THE COFFEE EXPERIENCE'

These discoveries may be exciting for the bean-geek roasters, but they're also satisfying their customers' increased appetite for single origins. In a bid to give coffee lovers the chance to sip amid the buzz of the roastery, a hangout space has been added to the in-house coffee bar where many of these single origins can be sampled.

Many other exceptional greens from across the coffee-growing belt are roasted at Heartland, including Great Taste award-winners Landmark and Swiss Water Process Decaf Blend.

**Established**
2005

**Roaster make and size**
Coffee-Tech Ghibli 45kg, Coffee-Tech Ghibli 15kg

LLANDUDNO

CAFE ON SITE

OPEN BY INVITE

BUY BEANS ONLINE

BUY BEANS IN STORE

# 17 MUG RUN COFFEE

Unit E3 Morfa Clwyd, Marsh Road, Rhyl, Denbighshire, LL18 2AF

mug-run.com | 07772 784471

f *mug.run* ⊙ *mug_run*

The beating heart of this Denbighshire roastery is the people – from all corners of the globe – whose efforts in each step of the coffee process result in consciously produced (and ultra-tasty) beans.

The Mug Run team strive to ensure every one of those people is treated fairly in the coffee's journey from plant to cup. Beans are sourced from independent farmers across all coffee-growing continents, ethically imported, and then hand-roasted in Norma (the crew's 10kg roaster).

## 'THE BEATING HEART OF THIS DENBIGHSHIRE ROASTERY IS THE PEOPLE'

The result? Carefully curated and diverse roasts. The Shed Blend is a harmonious balance of flavour, delivering chocolatey fruit notes and a sweet finish. As much care is used when selecting their decaf, which is decaffeinated using the natural sparkling water method. If you like what you taste, you can set up a subscription for a monthly fix or book yourself onto a Mug Run Coffee course.

Human connection comes a little closer to home too, as the gang prioritise collaborating with and supporting other indies and makers. You'll catch them at local makers' markets and national food and coffee festivals.

**Established**
2013

**Roaster make and size**
Bespoke 10kg

COFFEE COURSES | BUY BEANS ONLINE | BUY BEANS IN STORE |  CYMRAEG

# WEST & MID WALES

**18** Abersoch

Enyri National Park

Aberystwyth

**28** Tanygroes

**19** Fishguard

**23**
**24**
**21**
**22**
Carmarthen
**27** Llandeilo

A48
Ammanford

Haverfordwest

**26**

Pembrokeshire
Coast National
Park

**20**

**25**

Llanelli

**29**

## ● CAFES

## ● ROASTERIES

Find more good cafes and roasteries on pages 108–111

*All locations are approximate*

# 18 TWO ISLANDS

Bank Place, Lon Pen Cei, Abersoch, Gwynedd, LL53 7DW

twoislandsicecream.co.uk | 07904 806218

*f twoislandsicecream* ⊙ *two__islands*

A former bank manager's office is the unlikely home of Two Islands, a sleek ice cream and coffee shop inspired by the parlours of America's West Coast.

Rich textures and full flavours come as standard here thanks to the use of the finest ingredients. The small-batch ice cream is free from commercial fillers and stabilisers, and the homemade cakes are made with seasonal fruits, vegetables and wholegrain flours.

## TIP ON SUNNY DAYS, ORDER AN AFFOGATO AND HEAD TO THE MEDITERRANEAN-INSPIRED GARDEN

Crowd-pleasing ice cream flavours include brown-sugar-roasted banana, peanut butter and blackcurrant jam, and salted coffee made with Coaltown Coffee espresso and flaky sea salt from Halen Môn on Anglesey.

Impressed with Coaltown's goods, the Two Islands team recently collaborated with the roastery to create a signature single-origin for the coffee shop. The winning roast is a natural Brazilian, a juicy coffee that pairs nicely with milk but also drinks well black. It's served alongside Coaltown's washed single-origin decaf Jenkin Jones.

**Established**
2018

**Key roaster**
Coaltown
Coffee Roastery

**Brewing method**
Espresso, cold brew

**Machine**
La Marzocco Linea
PB ABR

**Grinder**
Mahlkonig E80
Supreme

**Opening hours**
Thu–Mon
9am–4pm

**REUSABLES ACCEPTED**

**DOGS WELCOME**

**BUY BEANS IN STORE**

**OUTDOOR SEATING**

**CYMRAEG**

ABERSOCH

# 19 THE GOURMET PIG

32 West Street, Fishguard, Pembrokeshire, SA65 9AD
gourmetpig.co.uk | 01348 874404

*f gourmetpig* *@ gourmetpigcoffeeco*

Visitors to Fishguard seeking a decent cup of coffee are swiftly directed by locals to The Gourmet Pig, a speciality deli and coffee shop in the heart of the coastal town.

If the smell of freshly roasted coffee lures you through the door, it's the magnetic pull of piles of delicious artisanal produce that will entice you to linger longer. An assortment of chutneys, jams, olive oils, vinegars and wines line the shelves, while fresh breads, cheeses, salads, quiches and antipasti adorn the counter.

## TIP CHECK OUT THE RETAIL SHELVES FOR BAGS OF GOURMET PIG COFFEE BEANS TO TAKE HOME

The indoor seating area is small, but it's worth fighting for a seat so you can pick a vinyl to spin on the in-house turntable. Once you've selected your soundtrack, pair a doughy doorstep of ciabatta stuffed with Preseli Mountain-reared Dexter beef brisket, gruyère, cornichons and Toloja Orchards mustard with a cup of the deli's own Peru-Honduras blend.

The Gourmet Pig follows a low-food-mile philosophy, so many of the ingredients are sourced locally. They've also introduced a zero-waste stand where customers can stock up on refills of muesli, beans, pulses, nuts and coffee beans.

**Established**
2009

**Key roaster**
The Gourmet Pig
Coffee Co

**Brewing method**
Espresso, drip

**Machine**
Conti Monte Carlo

**Grinder**
Mahlkonig,
Mazzer Super
Jolly × 2

**Opening hours**
Mon-Fri
9.30am-4.30pm
Sat
9.30am-4pm

REUSABLES ACCEPTED | WIFI | BIKE FRIENDLY | DOGS WELCOME | BUY BEANS IN STORE | COFFEE COURSES | OUTDOOR SEATING

# 20 GET THE BOYS A LIFT

40 Bridge Street, Haverfordwest, Pembrokeshire, SA61 2AD
gtbal.co.uk
**f** *gettheboysalift* 🅾 *gettheboysalift*

Studio Loop

If you've ever felt guilty about the amount you spend on coffee then a trip to this cafe should clear your conscience. The community hub provides free counselling and mental-health support to people in the area, all of which is funded by the flat whites and merch sold in the GTBAL coffee shop.

The team sling 'spros from their La Marzocco Linea machine, transforming Allpress beans and local The Mount milk into velvety flat whites, cappuccinos and lattes. Pop in to pick up a takeaway coffee and browse the retail offering, which includes tees, hoodies and hats. In the cafe space you'll also spot a What's On board, filled with info on free services such as drug and alcohol support, CV-writing classes and work experience.

## TIP WANT TO SUPPORT GTBAL BUT CAN'T MAKE IT TO WEST WALES? MAKE A DONATION ONLINE

In 2022, a mobile coffee shop joined the GTBAL gang. The new van parks up at Freshwater West between April and October, and appears at festivals and events throughout the year. A La Marzocco Linea Mini and Mythos One grinder have the mobile baristas set to serve top-notch coffee on any terrain.

**Established**
2019

**Key roaster**
Allpress Espresso

**Brewing method**
Espresso

**Machine**
La Marzocco
Linea Classic

**Grinder**
Victoria Arduino
Mythos One

**Opening hours**
Mon-Fri
7.30am-4pm
Sat
9am-1pm

REUSABLES ACCEPTED    WIFI    DOGS WELCOME    BUY BEANS IN STORE    COFFEE COURSES

# 21 CAFFI'R ATOM

18 King Street, Carmarthen, Carmarthenshire, SA31 1BH
alfiescoffeeco.co.uk | 07730 366123
*f caffiratom ⓘ caffir_atom*

**C**affi'r Atom is more than just a space to enjoy good coffee; it's an opportunity to immerse yourself in the world of speciality. Owner, barista and roaster Paul Cammack is a coffee evangelist who relishes nothing more than sharing the art of the brew with his customers – whether that's explaining the importance of properly preparing a portafilter or revealing how a specific brewing method can enhance flavour profile. His aim? To inspire appreciation of the craft and elevate the customer experience.

## TIP TRY THE HOUSE FAVE GARLIC AND ROSEMARY FRIES

All the coffees served here are roasted by Paul at the house roastery, Alfie's, and the latest development is the introduction of a monthly special. Enjoyed as espresso or V60, the beans offer something totally different from the house blend (Great Taste award-winning Caleb's Roast) and are chosen to showcase different origins, processing methods and flavour profiles.

The care with which the team craft the coffee is mirrored in the food menu, which is stuffed with brunch dishes and deep-filled toasties (try the Philly cheesesteak – it's Paul's favourite).

**Established**
2021

**Key roaster**
Alfie's Coffee Company

**Brewing method**
Espresso, V60

**Machine**
La Marzocco Linea PB

**Grinder**
Mahlkonig K30 ES

**Opening hours**
Mon–Fri
10am–3pm

**REUSABLES ACCEPTED**

**WIFI**

**DOGS WELCOME**

**BUY BEANS IN STORE**

**COFFEE COURSES**

**OUTDOOR SEATING**

**CYMRAEG**

CARMARTHEN

51

# 22 HMY

41-45 Richmond Terrace, Carmarthen, Carmarthenshire, SA31 1HG

hmycustoms.co.uk | 07720 378852

f *hmycustoms* @ *hmy_customs*

**P**art coffee house, part custom artwork and clothing brand, HMY is where founder Hammy Darbyshire's interests in colour, coffee and community collide.

After running their custom painting company for several years, in 2023 Hammy and team moved the operation to roomier digs so they could expand the business and throw a coffee element into the mix. Now customers can ogle the kaleidoscopic custom boots, shoes and jerseys (they specialise in all things two-wheeled) in the coffee house while sipping a single origin.

## TIP GIGANTIC TRAYBAKES AND BROWNIES FUEL THE CYCLISTS WHO MAKE A PIT STOP

The beans are roasted by Bay Coffee in Cardigan and then transformed into on-point espresso drinks by the baristas, who are latte art pros. Flat whites are often adorned with swans while hot chocolates for little ones reveal elephants.

There's a real community feel to the coffee house; it's not only popular with cyclists and bikers but also with local families. On the wall you'll spot a VIPup board (with pics of four-pawed visitors) and a community cork wall where you can snap a polaroid and leave a message.

**Established**
2023

**Key roaster**
Bay Coffee Roasters

**Brewing method**
Espresso

**Machine**
La Marzocco

**Grinder**
Anfim, Compak

**Opening hours**
Mon-Fri
8am-5pm
Sat-Sun
8am-4pm

REUSABLES ACCEPTED | WIFI | BIKE FRIENDLY | DOGS WELCOME | BUY BEANS IN STORE | COFFEE COURSES | OUTDOOR SEATING | CYMRAEG

CARMARTHEN

52

# 23 DIOD

135 Rhosmaen Street, Llandeilo, Carmarthenshire, SA19 6EN

diod.cymru | 01558 824023

*f diodllandeilo* *◎ diodllandeilo*

Those learning Cymraeg will know that 'diod' translates as 'drink' in English, and this Welsh coffee shop with Scandi vibes is a great place to practise your pronunciation and sip coffee that's been roasted in Wales.

Ninety per cent of the team speak Welsh so Diod is a great place to soak up the Cymraeg vibe, whether you're a native speaker or a newbie. However, whichever language you choose to order in, you'll receive a warm welcome from the friendly baristas.

Coffee fuelling the multilingual chatter is roasted by the pros at Gower Coffee in Swansea, and the house serve is a bespoke blend crafted especially for Diod. Owner Lisa and the crew recently invested in a second grinder so they could introduce guest beans to the line-up.

## TIP FEELING THE HEAT? COOL DOWN WITH AN AFFOGATO

A small menu of breakfasts, light bites, sandwiches and cakes is served throughout the day, and in the afternoon a list of good wines (including Welsh drops) is available as an alternative to the coffee offering. Fully loaded retail shelves give visitors the option to pick up coffee beans and wine to take home.

**Established**
2021

**Key roaster**
Gower Coffee

**Brewing method**
Espresso

**Machine**
Fracino Contempo

**Grinder**
Sanremo SR70

**Opening hours**
Mon–Thu
9am–5pm
Fri–Sat
9am–6pm

**WIFI**  **DOGS WELCOME**  **BUY BEANS IN STORE**  **CYMRAEG**

# 24 PITCHFORK & PROVISION

Castle Courtyard, 113 Rhosmaen Street, Llandeilo, Carmarthenshire, SA19 6HN

pitchforkandprovision.wales | 07886 447276

f pitchforkandprovision  @ pitchfork.and.provision

Sourdough and speciality coffee, arguably two of life's greatest pleasures, are the star serves at this cafe-bakery in Llandeilo. Both go through laborious processes to end up in customers' hands, where they're swiftly devoured in mere minutes.

Each perfectly risen loaf is made from scratch over the course of 36 hours by the Pitchfork & Provision bakers. Their foolproof recipe uses a ten-year-old levain starter and a blend of Shipton Mill white, wholemeal and rye flours, plus a little sea salt and water. Once ready, the homemade bakes are used as the base of a multitude of vibrant brunch dishes such as croissant french toast with banana, Biscoff and salted-caramel sauce.

## TIP DON'T MISS THE REGULAR PIZZA NIGHTS

The house espresso, a single-origin washed coffee from Sidamo in Ethiopia, is lightly roasted by the pros at Coaltown Coffee Roasters. It was specifically handpicked by the P&P team to complement the distinctive flavours of the house sourdough, as well as the ever-changing array of pastries and sweet bakes that line the counter.

After polishing off a flat white and plate of french toast, explore the deli selection stocked with artisan cheeses, drinks and dried goods.

**Established**
2020

**Key roaster**
Coaltown Coffee
Roastery

**Brewing method**
Espresso

**Machine**
La Marzocco GB5 S

**Grinder**
Mahlkonig E65S
GbW

**Opening hours**
Seasonal opening
hours

LLANDEILO

**REUSABLES ACCEPTED**

**WIFI**

**BIKE FRIENDLY**

**DOGS WELCOME**

**BUY BEANS IN STORE**

**OUTDOOR SEATING**

**CYMRAEG**

# 25 COALTOWN ESPRESSO BAR

The Roastery, Foundry Road, Ammanford, Carmarthenshire, SA18 2LS

coaltowncoffee.co.uk | 01269 400105

**f** *coaltowncoffeeroasters* **◎** *coaltowncoffee*

Coffee fans exploring Wales might expect to find a good coffee shop or two in a town this far west, but to encounter a speciality roastery with training academy and espresso bar is somewhat surprising.

Coaltown's open-plan HQ on the outskirts of Ammanford is a busy hive of caffeinated activity. As well as hosting its roastery, which supplies cafes, restaurants and indie businesses across Wales with top-flight beans, it's the home of Coaltown's espresso bar and training space where locals and visitors gather to try the goods and learn how to prepare them at home.

## TIP JOIN ONE OF THE WORKSHOPS (ESPRESSO AND LATTE ART, OR FILTER) AT THE TRAINING ACADEMY

Make the trip to sample the latest house blends and single origins while watching the roasters rustle up the next batch. Black Gold is the house espresso blend and where the Coaltown story began in 2014; the current version is the third iteration of the blend and a great place for first timers to start.

Securing B Corp status for the business in 2019, founder Scott James has always been passionate about his local community and created the Ammanford hub in his hometown in order to employ people from this rural area.

**Established**
2014

**Key roaster**
Coaltown Coffee Roastery

**Brewing method**
Espresso

**Machine**
La Marzocco KB90

**Grinder**
Mahlkonig EK43,
Mahlkonig E65S × 2

**Opening hours**
Mon–Sun
8am–4pm

**REUSABLES ACCEPTED**

**WIFI**

**BIKE FRIENDLY**

**DOGS WELCOME**

**BUY BEANS IN STORE**

**COFFEE COURSES**

**OUTDOOR SEATING**

**CYMRAEG**

# 26 HUMBLE COFFI

Unit 2 Stradey District Centre, Sandy Road, Llanelli, Carmarthenshire, SA15 4EB

humblecoffi.com

*f humblecoffi* *@ humblecoffi*

L ocated a stone's throw from the former Stradey Park stadium, this unassuming coffee house is an insider's find for good coffee and cafe food.

The team focus on quality, but that doesn't mean the vibe is pretentious: this is a relaxed, friendly spot where customers can sip a velvety espresso or appreciate the flavours of a well-prepared AeroPress at a leisurely pace. Coffee fans, yoga mums, retirees and youngsters all enjoy the industrial-style space.

## TIP VISIT ON A SATURDAY EVENING FOR TAPAS AND COCKTAILS

If you're dithering over which dish to sample from the all-day menu, the house special of waffles stacked with buttermilk fried chicken, bacon and maple syrup is happiness on a plate. Craving something lighter? Order the smoked salmon sourdough, slathered with cream cheese and sprinkled with pink pickled onions and dukkah.

Leave room to treat yourself to one of the tempting doughnuts stacked in the bakery cabinet. Resistance is futile when faced with flavours such as apple crumble, blackcurrant and lemon crunch, and white chocolate, fudge and raspberry.

**Established**
2019

**Key roaster**
Clifton Coffee Roasters

**Brewing method**
Espresso, filter, AeroPress

**Machine**
La Marzocco Linea Classic

**Grinder**
Mahlkonig E65

**Opening hours**
Mon, Thu-Fri
7.30am-4pm
Sat
7.30am-10.30pm
Sun
10am-4pm

REUSABLES
ACCEPTED

WIFI

BIKE
FRIENDLY

BUY BEANS
IN STORE

COFFEE
COURSES

CYMRAEG

# 27 SHIRE COFFEE AT HWYL

20 Market Street, Llanelli, Carmarthenshire, SA15 1YD

shire.coffee | 01554 775537

**f** *shirecoffeeco* ⊙ *hwyl.shire*

In February 2023, the team behind Llanelli's roaming coffee shop took over the town's esteemed brunch spot, and Shire Coffee at Hwyl was born. The Shire gang knew not to mess with a good thing so, instead of reinventing the wheel, simply slid their elevated coffee offering in alongside Hwyl's much-loved brunch line-up.

The Shire van continues to pitch up at Sandy Water Park from Thursday to Saturday, but for a more formal fix fans can now also get it at the cafe in town. At both venues, there's a house blend from Coaltown alongside guest roasts from the likes of Ue, Round Hill and Skylark, showcasing the diversity of the speciality scene.

### TIP THE BARISTAS ARE PASSIONATE ABOUT BREWING INTERESTING COFFEES – ASK THEM WHAT'S IN THE HOPPER WHEN YOU VISIT

Perennially popular brunch dishes are served all day and include the likes of banana bread with berry compote, crème fraîche, peanut butter and chia seeds, and smashed avo with smoked salmon, poached eggs and sourdough. If you like what you're eating, book a seat at one of the regular pop-up evenings which cover a globetrotting array of cuisines.

**Established**
2023

**Key roaster**
Coaltown Coffee
Roastery

**Brewing method**
Espresso,
batch filter,
cold brew

**Machine**
La Marzocco
Linea PB

**Grinder**
Mahlkonig E65S,
Mazzer Major V

**Opening hours**
Tue–Sat
9am–3pm

REUSABLES ACCEPTED   WIFI   DOGS WELCOME   BUY BEANS IN STORE   OUTDOOR SEATING   CYMRAEG

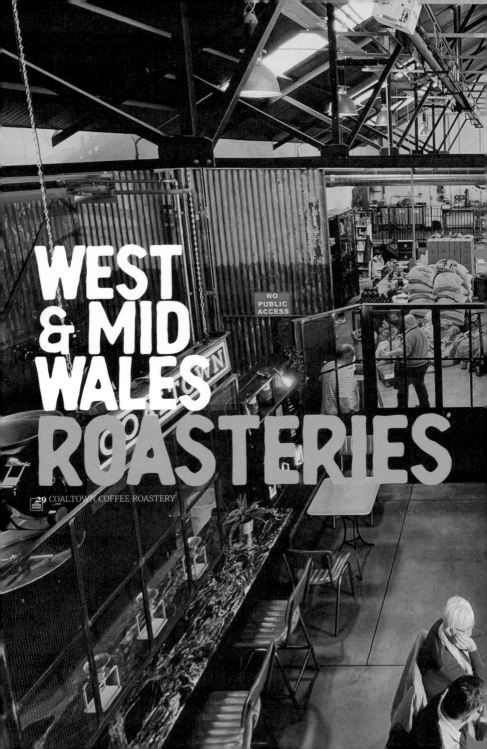

# WEST
# & MID
# WALES
# ROASTERIES

**29** COALTOWN COFFEE ROASTERY

# 28 BAY COFFEE ROASTERS

Unit 2 Parc Tanygroes, Tanygroes, Ceredigion, SA43 2JP

baycoffeeroasters.com | 01239 814550

*f welshcoffee* ⊙ *baycoffeeroasters*

Powered by 100 per cent renewable energy, this Ceredigion roastery is making waves in the coffee industry for its planet-forward approach.

At the Roast Masters 2023 competition in Amsterdam, Bay Coffee stood out from the crowd as the only roastery to run on green energy. The team got to the quarter finals (going further than any other UK roastery) and even achieved a higher score than the previous year's winner. Further praise for their eco practices includes getting to the finals of The Wales Food and Drink Awards in the Sustainable Values category.

While owner Duncan Gray and team are steadfast in their commitment to reducing the business' environmental impact, they don't want it to be all the brand is known for. Bay Coffee beans are also famous for their flavour, which has scooped them a plethora of Great Taste awards including a Golden Fork (the highest Great Taste accolade).

## 'MAKING WAVES IN THE COFFEE INDUSTRY FOR ITS PLANET-FRIENDLY APPROACH'

Beans are sourced via ethical importers and, once landed at the Tanygroes HQ, are bronzed using one of four electric roasters. A recent direct partnership with Diego of Sonora Coffee in Costa Rica (who uses hydropower at his farm and mill) has resulted in an exciting release that's as ethically sound as it is delicious.

**Established**
2011

**Roaster make and size**
Coffee Crafters Artisan X-e 4kg × 2, Rubasse 3kg × 2, Aillio Bullet R1 1kg, IKAWA Pro100

BUY BEANS ONLINE

CYMRAEG

TANYGROES

# 29 COALTOWN COFFEE ROASTERY

The Roastery, Foundry Road, Ammanford, Camarthenshire, SA18 2LS

coaltowncoffee.co.uk | 01269 400105

*f* coaltowncoffeeroasters @ coaltowncoffee

**T**he first speciality coffee roastery in the UK to earn B Corp status wasn't based in London, Manchester or even Cardiff, but in the former mining town of Ammanford in Carmarthenshire.

When Scott James established Coaltown Coffee in 2014, his founding principle was to put people and purpose above profit. Once his coffee brand had built momentum, he decided to establish the company's open-plan roastery, espresso bar and training academy in his hometown in order to provide jobs for locals who struggled to find work in this rural location.

## 'PEOPLE AND PURPOSE ABOVE PROFIT'

The industrial-style HQ is where Coaltown's broad list of blends and single origins is roasted. The longstanding house blend, Black Gold, is on its third phase and is currently an intoxicating mix of beans from Brazil, Peru and El Salvador. For those after something more adventurous, there's a shifting selection of single origins chosen for their bright and interesting flavour profiles.

If you're in the area, a visit to the espresso bar in the roastery is a must. Those who can't make it out west can enjoy the Coaltown experience at home via the newly improved subscription service.

**Established**
2014

**Roaster make and size**
Probat GG75 75kg,
Probat 12kg

CAFE
ON SITE

OPEN TO
THE PUBLIC

COFFEE
COURSES

BUY BEANS
ONLINE

BUY BEANS
IN STORE

CYMRAEG

# SOUTH WALES

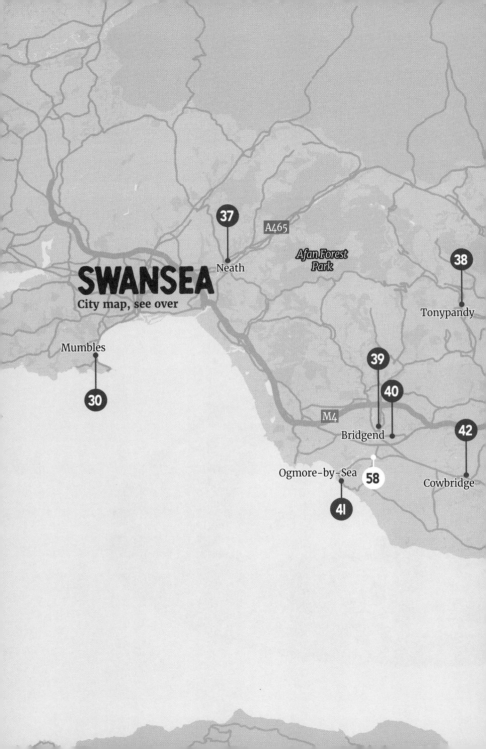

**57** Abergavenny

A40

**60**

A465

Ebbw Vale

A40

A4042

**56**

Blackwood

A470

**55**

**59**

Caerphilly

M4

# CARDIFF
**City map, see over**

Penarth

**43**

Barry

**44**

## ● CAFES

## ○ ROASTERIES

Find more good cafes and roasteries on pages
108–111

*All locations are approximate

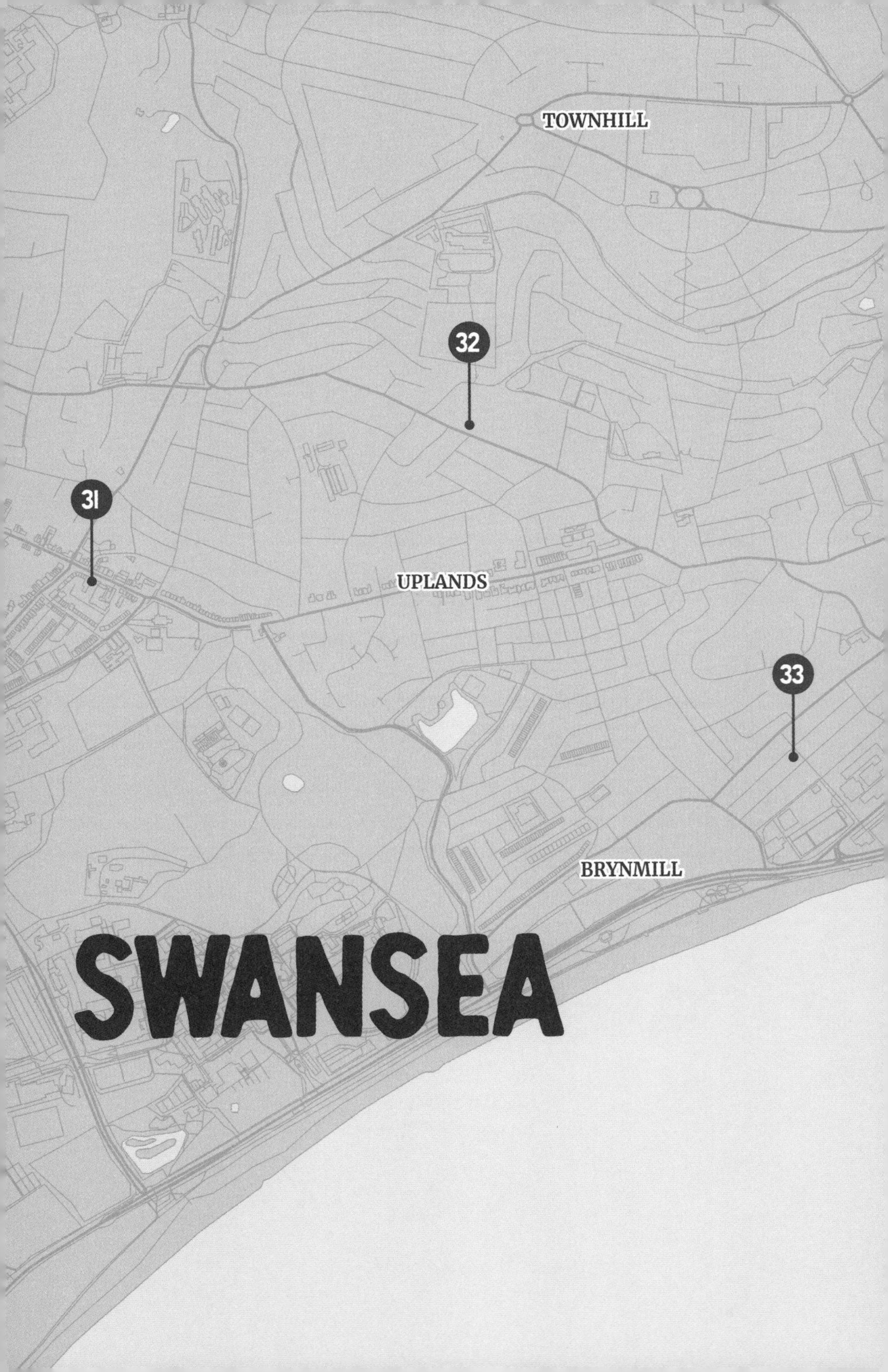

TOWNHILL

32

31

UPLANDS

33

BRYNMILL

# SWANSEA

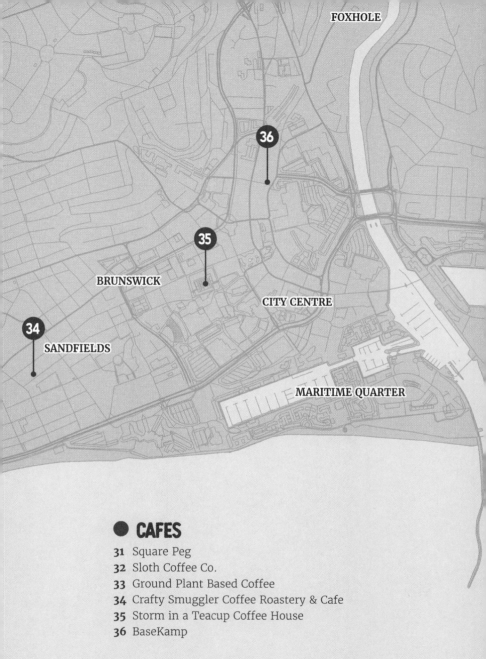

FOXHOLE

**36**

**35**

BRUNSWICK

CITY CENTRE

**34**

SANDFIELDS

MARITIME QUARTER

## ● CAFES

Find more good cafes and roasteries on pages 108–111

*All locations are approximate*

HEATH

54

53

52

51

CATHAYS

PONTCANNA

50

48

49

RIVERSIDE

VICTORIA
PARK

47

CITY CENTRE

46

BUTETOWN

61

45

# CARDIFF

## ● CAFES

## ● TRAINER

Find more good cafes and roasteries on pages 108–111

*All locations are approximate*

# 30 MICROLOT BY MUMBLES COFFEE

28 Dunns Lane, Mumbles, Swansea, SA3 4AA

mumblescoffee.co.uk

🖸 microlot

Set back from the seafront between pastel-coloured fishing cottages, Microlot is the perfect place to escape the crowds and savour a cup of expertly prepared coffee from Bristol's Extract.

Opened in 2021, the little sister venue to Mumbles Coffee continues the family tradition of pairing fantastic speciality coffee with freshly baked pastries.

Extract's house espresso, prepared on a Modbar AV, is joined by guest beans from other top roasteries such as Outpost, Poblado and Heartland, with V60 pourover also available. You can buy beans to-go too, which can be ground to your specification.

### TIP GOWER DOUGHNUT CO. DELIVERS ON FRIDAYS AND SATURDAYS. NEED WE SAY MORE?

When the weather's good, the glass panels are removed from the windows, allowing the sea breeze to stir souls and coffee aromas. Pull up a pew outside for full-on sun worshipping with a fresh-fruit smoothie. On the (admittedly more likely) occasions when it rains, snuggle up inside on a window seat and soak up the laid-back vibe.

**Established**
2021

**Key roaster**
Extract Coffee Roasters

**Brewing method**
Espresso, V60

**Machine**
La Marzocco Modbar AV

**Grinder**
Mahlkonig EK43, Mahlkonig E65S GbW × 2

**Opening hours**
Mon-Sat
8am-3pm

SWANSEA

REUSABLES ACCEPTED   WIFI   BIKE FRIENDLY   DOGS WELCOME   BUY BEANS IN STORE   OUTDOOR SEATING   CYMRAEG

# 31 SQUARE PEG

29b Gower Road, Sketty, Swansea, SA2 9BX
squarepeg.org.uk | 01792 206593
**f** *squarepegcoffee* **◎** *squarepegcoffee*

This longstanding community space was established to do things differently. As the first speciality coffee shop in Swansea, the Square Peg team raised the bar for quality caffeine in the city while also paying back to their local area by donating profits to Zac's Place, a charity that supports homeless people.

Over the past eight years, founders Matt and Claire Crome have worked with their team to continually improve the cafe's coffee offering. They've collaborated with a Welsh roastery to create a custom roast and have developed their own canned cold brew, which can be sampled in-house or taken home to enjoy later.

## TIP BOOK ONTO AN SCA-ACCREDITED BARISTA COURSE AT THE SQUARE PEG COFFEE ACADEMY

The food offering is as special as the coffee. The team recently collaborated with a local grower to supply the kitchen with sustainable organic ingredients, which the clever chefs transform into tasty dishes such as the veggie masala brunch. When locals hear the specials board has been updated, they rush down to roadtest the latest dish. Join them to tuck into the likes of burrata with heritage tomatoes, and buffalo corn ribs with ranch dressing.

**Established**
2015

**Key roaster**
Coaltown Coffee Roastery

**Brewing method**
Espresso, batch filter, cold brew

**Machine**
La Marzocco Linea PB

**Grinder**
Mahlkonig EK43, Victoria Arduino Mythos One

**Opening hours**
Mon–Wed
8am–2pm
Thu–Sat
8am–3.30pm

**REUSABLES ACCEPTED**

**WIFI**

**BIKE FRIENDLY**

**DOGS WELCOME**

**BUY BEANS IN STORE**

**COFFEE COURSES**

**OUTDOOR SEATING**

# 32 SLOTH COFFEE CO.

102 Glanmor Road, Swansea, SA2 0QB

07759 506441

sloth.coffee.co

Step inside Sloth Coffee and the laid-back vibe will quickly answer any questions you may have about the name above the door. Just months after opening it's already one of the city's most popular places to chill, with owners (and brothers) Harry and Dai making a big impact on the community in which they grew up.

With backgrounds in carpentry, the duo built Sloth from the ground up, and similar attention to detail has been paid to the coffee. The house espresso is Odd Kin's full-bodied Treehouse blend, and there are single origins from a constantly shifting line-up of roasteries on the batch filter menu and retail shelves.

## TIP ARRIVE EARLY TO SECURE ONE OF SLOTH'S FAMOUS MONSTER COOKIES

The eating is as good as the drinking: people travel from across Swansea for Sloth's homemade veggie sausage rolls. In summer, pair one with a fresh fruit-infused iced tea.

Don't miss the Sloth Den, a small retail space providing customers with a slice of the experience to take home – check out the branded refillable coffee jars and graphic tees.

**Established**
2022

**Key roaster**
Odd Kin
Coffee Roasters

**Brewing method**
Espresso, V60,
batch filter,
AeroPress,
cold brew

**Machine**
Victoria Arduino
Eagle One

**Grinder**
Mahlkonig EK43,
Victoria Arduino
Mythos One,
Victoria Arduino
MYG75

**Opening hours**
Mon-Fri
7am-2pm
Sat
8am-2pm

SWANSEA

REUSABLES
ACCEPTED

WIFI

BIKE
FRIENDLY

DOGS
WELCOME

BUY BEANS
IN STORE

COFFEE
COURSES

OUTDOOR
SEATING

# 33 GROUND PLANT BASED COFFEE

The Sup Hut, Francis Street, Swansea, SA1 4NH
greatgreenkitchen.com | 07581 005605

**f** *groundcoffeeswansea* **◎** *groundswansea*

Nothing rouses the appetite like a paddleboard session in choppy waves, so the installation of this speciality coffee shop within The Sup Hut (the home of all things SUP, a stone's throw from Swansea Beach) was a genius idea from Helen Wilson of Great Green Kitchen and paddleboard pro Matt Barker-Smith.

Paddlers still salty from the surf can drop off their hire boards at the shop before reviving themselves with an expertly prepared Extract coffee. There are usually three options on offer from the Bristol roastery: Original Espresso (caramel, cocoa and hazelnut), Decaf (fruit loaf, cocoa and caramel) and a seasonal guest such as Unkle Funka (blood orange marmalade, Jammie Dodger and cardamom).

## TIP PICK UP A COFFEE TO-GO AND TAKE A SCENIC STROLL ALONG THE BEACH

Following the coffee shop's vegan principles, milk-based coffees are served with oat as standard but soy and coconut alternatives are also available. If you're looking for something even more restorative, check out the line-up of specialist hot drinks which include medicinal mushroom lattes.

Savoury bites and homemade bakes are piled on the counter and include the likes of orange and almond polenta cake and Portuguese-style custard tarts.

**Established**
2021

**Key roaster**
Extract
Coffee Roasters

**Brewing method**
Espresso

**Machine**
La Marzocco
Linear Classic

**Grinder**
Compak F8

**Opening hours**
Mon, Fri
8.30am–3pm
Tue–Thu
8.30am–2.30pm
Sat
9am–2pm

**REUSABLES ACCEPTED**

**BUY BEANS IN STORE**

**OUTDOOR SEATING**

**CYMRAEG**

SWANSEA

73

# 34 CRAFTY SMUGGLER COFFEE ROASTERY & CAFE

82a Western Street, Sandfields, Swansea, SA1 3JS
craftysmugglercoffee.co.uk | 07402 018835
*f craftysmugglercoffee* *craftysmugglercoffee*

There aren't many places in Swansea where you can savour a coffee that's been roasted in the city, so be sure to pin this cafe-roastery on your mobile maps.

From a tiny coffee shop housed in a former garage, the Crafty Smuggler baristas brew super-fresh coffee using beans from their roastery across town. Play it safe (but smart) by opting for house espresso The Full Barrel, a smooth blend of El Salvadorian, Ethiopian and Colombian beans. It yields notes of cocoa and nuts when paired with milk, and hints of orange when served black. If you're up for something different, ask about the latest single-origin release for a palate-expanding experience.

## TIP PICK UP A BAG OF CRAFTY SMUGGLER BEANS FOR YOUR HOME HOPPER

The coffee shop has a smattering of indoor and outdoor seating, from which you can leisurely sip your pick of the coffee menu and tuck into one of the sweet or savoury bakes from the countertop selection.

**Established**
2023

**Key roaster**
Crafty Smuggler Coffee

**Brewing method**
Espresso

**Machine**
Conti Monte Carlo

**Grinder**
Eureka Zenith

**Opening hours**
Mon-Fri
8am-4pm
Sat-Sun
9am-3pm

SWANSEA

REUSABLES
ACCEPTED    WIFI    BIKE
FRIENDLY    DOGS
WELCOME    BUY BEANS
IN STORE    OUTDOOR
SEATING    CYMRAEG

# 35 STORM IN A TEACUP COFFEE HOUSE

Stall 59, Swansea Market, Union Street, Swansea, SA1 3PQ

07967 980778

f storminateacupcoffeehouse  ⊚ storminateacupcoffeehouse

No trip to Swansea Market is complete without swinging by Storm in a Teacup to see what's brewing. In fact, as speciality is in short supply on this side of town, the tiny espresso and brew bar is the reason many local coffee fans make the trip to Wales' largest indoor market.

Whether you make a planned pit stop or enjoy a chance encounter, a belter of a brew and a friendly chinwag with founder Ian Curtis awaits. Drawing on his 30 years of barista experience, Ian fashions beans from London's Square Mile into glossy espresso and batch brew.

## TIP TAKE YOUR REUSABLE CUP (OR 'SMUG GOBLET', AS IAN CALLS IT) FOR A SWEET DISCOUNT

If the weather's warm and a hot drink doesn't appeal, the fruit-packed iced teas and affogatos are deliciously refreshing alternatives. However, the daily changing line-up of bakes (including gooey brownies and syrupy flapjacks) from local makers are year-round delights to pair with your drink.

**Established**
2019

**Key roaster**
Square Mile
Coffee Roasters

**Brewing method**
Espresso,
batch filter

**Machine**
Victoria Arduino
Black Eagle

**Grinder**
Victoria Arduino
Mythos One,
Mahlkonig EK43

**Opening hours**
Mon–Sat
8am–4pm

REUSABLES
ACCEPTED

BIKE
FRIENDLY

DOGS
WELCOME

BUY BEANS
IN STORE

SWANSEA

# 36 BASEKAMP

The Warehouse, Kings Lane, Swansea, SA1 2AQ

07833 208595

f *basekampswansea* ⓘ *basekampswansea*

**B**ase camps provide a welcome pit stop for weary adventurers, which is a fitting description of this inviting coffee house within a converted warehouse.

It's popular with remote workers, students and flagging coffee fans who settle into the calming Scandi-style interior to tackle emails, catch up with friends or simply unwind. Cosy sofas, open-plan seating and abundant electrical sockets make it a great alternative to working from home.

## TIP RESIDENT DOG DYLAN IS ALWAYS AROUND FOR A CUDDLE, EXCEPT ON SUNDAYS – HIS DAY OFF

However, the most alluring thing about this Swansea hub is the coffee. The team at Clifton Coffee supply a reliably delicious house roast, while beans from Round Hill in Somerset make regular guest appearances on filter. If you order an espresso drink, you can watch it being prepared on the Conti Monte Carlo machine that sits on Basekamp's quirky tuk-tuk bar.

Don't leave without getting your chops round one of the freshly baked cakes or all-day brunch dishes. And be sure to explore the retail selection of beans from the likes of Extract, Hard Lines and Girls Who Grind.

**Established**
2020

**Key roaster**
Clifton Coffee Roasters

**Brewing method**
Espresso, V60, french press, cold brew, batch filter

**Machine**
Conti Monte Carlo

**Grinder**
Mahlkonig EK43

**Opening hours**
Mon-Fri
9am-5pm
Sat-Sun
10am-5pm
(seasonal opening hours)

REUSABLES ACCEPTED

WIFI

BIKE FRIENDLY

DOGS WELCOME

BUY BEANS IN STORE

COFFEE COURSES

OUTDOOR SEATING

# 37 MONTY'S

Unit 5 Shufflebotham Lane, Neath, SA11 3FJ

07471 087423

*f* *Monty's Coffee Neath*  *⊙* *montyscoffeeneath*

Launched in November 2020, Monty's was a roaming coffee shop for its first two years in business. After building a fanbase serving espresso from a converted van across Wales' south coast, owner Mathew Davies found the perfect home in Neath.

Named after the Davies' family dachshund, Monty's has quickly settled into new surroundings with a coffee offering to rival any cafe in the area. The South American house blend is roasted by Welsh heavyweights Coaltown, while in the second and third grinders you'll find Clifton's El Salvador E1 and Hard Lines' celebrated Colombia El Carmen.

## 🆃🅸🅿 ORDER THE QUAD-SHOT 'FLAT WHITE TURBO' AND BUCKLE UP FOR A WILD RIDE

Pick up a fresh, locally baked Pitchfork & Provision pastry on your way through and, if you've timed it right, a seasonal serve to go with it – pumpkin spiced lattes in jacket weather, affogato and iced coffees when the mercury rises.

A partnership with independent dairy Daisy Bank means you can buy a bottle of organic milk and return to refill it - not that anyone needs an excuse to come back to this thriving community-focused coffee spot.

**Established**
2022

**Key roaster**
Coaltown Coffee
Roastery

**Brewing method**
Espresso,
batch filter

**Machine**
La Marzocco Linea
Classic S

**Grinder**
Mahlkonig E65S
GbW × 3

**Opening hours**
Mon, Wed–Fri
7am–4pm
Sat
8am–3pm
Sun
8am–1pm

**REUSABLES ACCEPTED**  **WIFI**  **BIKE FRIENDLY**  **DOGS WELCOME**  **BUY BEANS IN STORE**  **OUTDOOR SEATING**

# 38 CLWB COFFI

Dunraven Street, Tonypandy, Rhondda Cynon Taff, CF40 1AS
clwbcoffi.com
**f** *clwbcoffi* **◎** *clwbcoffi*

Once a thriving mining community, Tonypandy has twice been given the title of Wales' worst high street. Coffee-obsessed John Sutton grew tired of his hometown being written off and, with wife Sarah, set about changing the narrative.

The Suttons opened Clwb Coffi in August 2020 and, despite navigating the turbulent trading conditions of the pandemic, in 2021 it was named as the Welsh Innovation Centre for Enterprise startup of the year. Their vision to help kickstart a new chapter for their maligned community was becoming a reality.

## TIP KEEP AN EYE OPEN FOR REGULAR COLLABS WITH LOCAL STREET-FOOD VENDORS

The coffee and food offering hints at why this popular spot has been a runaway success. Origin's rich, chocolatey Brazilian Stronghold is the house blend and the perfect partner to delicious menu staples such as fluffy American-style pancakes and Sarah's chocolate brownies.

Clwb's Suspended Coffee scheme gives customers the opportunity to pay a coffee forward via a token system, providing hot drinks for those who might not be able to afford one themselves.

**Established**
2020

**Key roaster**
Origin Coffee
Roasters

**Brewing method**
Espresso,
batch filter

**Machine**
La Marzocco
Linea PB

**Grinder**
Mahlkonig EK43,
Victoria Arduino
Mythos One

**Opening hours**
Mon-Fri
8.30am-4pm
Sat
10am-3pm

REUSABLES ACCEPTED | WIFI | BIKE FRIENDLY | DOGS WELCOME | BUY BEANS IN STORE | COFFEE COURSES | OUTDOOR SEATING | CYMRAEG

# 39 BEAT BAKEHOUSE

1a Station Hill, Bridgend, CF31 1EA
beatbakehouse.com | 01656 530801
*f beatbakehouse* *◎ beatbakehouse*

In July 2022, Hollie and Adrian Moses introduced Bridgend's coffee drinkers to a new rhythm when they launched Beat Bakehouse and brought locally roasted speciality coffee, brilliant bakes and Nordic interiors to the town.

While the house coffee (Coaltown's rich and velvety Black Gold blend) is exceptional, the stars of the show here are the house-baked breads, pastries and cakes. From fully loaded seasonal sourdough focaccia sandwiches and giant sausage rolls to pumpkin pie and chocolate babka, there's something to appeal to every palate. The extensive food offering regularly features plant-based treats too – time your visit right and you might be in for a slice of sumptuous vegan chocolate gâteau.

## TIP BEAT HAS REMOVED ALL SINGLE-USE PLASTIC, SO ORDER IN AND CHILL OUT

Don't leave without grabbing something delicious to brew at home. Take your pick from beans roasted by Cardiff's Hard Lines and Gloucestershire's Rave, or grab a box of Coaltown's Nespresso-compatible pods.

**Established**
2022

**Key roaster**
Coaltown
Coffee Roastery

**Brewing method**
Espresso

**Machine**
La Marzocco
Linea PB ABV

**Grinder**
Mahlkonig EK43,
Mahlkonig E65
GbW

**Opening hours**
Mon–Fri
6.30am–3pm
Sat
8am–1pm

REUSABLES ACCEPTED | WIFI | DOGS WELCOME | BUY BEANS IN STORE | OUTDOOR SEATING

# GREAT COFFEE SHOPS DESERVE GREAT CAKE.

@cakesmiths.hq

## TRY US FOR FREE IN YOUR COFFEE SHOP!

- Award winning wholesale cakes

- Top-notch coffee shop solutions, with tips to maximise sales

- Loyalty points and free cake

- Unrivalled cake innovation from our Cake Lab

- New savoury scones and muffins

- Next day delivery, 6 days a week

- Eco-friendly packaging

- Everything made by hand

TRY US FOR FREE AT CAKESMITHS.COM/TRY-US

# 40 WHOCULT COFFEE + DONUTS

Unit 1d Kingsway Buildings, Bridgend Industrial Estate, Bridgend, CF31 3YH

whocult.com | 01656 648537

𝑓 *whocult* 📷 *whocult*

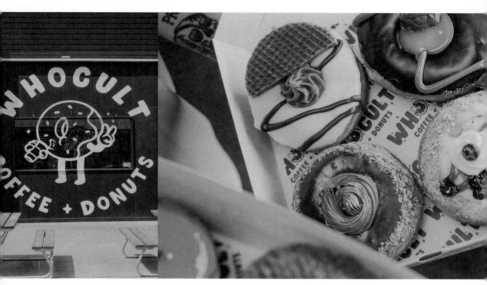

**E**ighty seconds was all it took for Whocult to sell 2,000 doughnuts online during lockdown. No flash in the pan, this brainchild of established Bridgend independent streetwear brand Whoclo has people travelling from as far as Essex for its doughy goods.

No one can argue with the team's claim of *'doughnuts bigger than your head'* as everything here is larger than life. A core of Whocult classics (Biscoff, Bueno, Reese's and Homer chocolate) are complemented by a regularly refreshed selection of limited editions – some seasonal, some just because.

## TIP CHECK OUT THE SISTER SITES IN BARRY, NEWPORT AND PORTHCAWL

If you're up to the challenge, pay a visit to the bakery HQ and match your pick with a milkshake. Or have a cup of Whocult's house coffee, a choc-nut-forward blend from El Salvador. If you like what you're sipping, grab a bag of beans to take home.

These doughnut dons also have special occasions covered: customise bakes with a message in icing or even ask them to replicate your favourite design – the possibilities are endless!

**Established**
2019

**Key roaster**
Welsh Coffee Co.

**Brewing method**
Espresso,
batch filter

**Machine**
La Spaziale S5

**Grinder**
Anfim Pratica

**Opening hours**
Mon-Sat
10am-6pm
Sun
10am-4pm

WIFI  BIKE FRIENDLY  DOGS WELCOME  BUY BEANS IN STORE  OUTDOOR SEATING

# 41 WELSH COFFEE COMMUNITY COFFEE SHOP

Community Hall, Slon Lane, Ogmore-by-Sea, Vale of Glamorgan, CF32 0PN

welshcoffee.com | 07900 011244

f *welshcoffee* ⓞ *welshcoffeeco*

**C**offee lovers following the Wales Coast Path through Ogmore-by-Sea will be thankful for this new addition to the seaside village.

The Welsh Coffee Co. (WCC) crew have been roasting in this corner of South Wales since 2011, but this venue within the village's futuristic community hall (the metal-clad entrance looks like something from a spaceship) is their first foray into the coffee-shop wing of the speciality industry. It's a fantastic spot for adventurers taking a break from the trail, with its sprawling sea views and comfy furniture fashioned from ocean plastic and spent coffee grounds.

## TIP IN GOOD WEATHER, YOU'LL FIND THE TEAM SLINGING SHOTS ON THE BEACH FROM THE WCC TRUCK

A coffee menu of espresso and pourover options is crafted from own-roasted beans, many of which are Great Taste winners. Blends Môr and Bendigedig have both been awarded two stars from the prestigious organisation, and are available to sample as espresso drinks. Single origins from Central and South America are best enjoyed via AeroPress or Chemex.

**Established**
2023

**Key roaster**
Welsh Coffee Co.

**Brewing method**
Espresso,
AeroPress, Chemex

**Machine**
La Marzocco Strada

**Grinder**
Anfim

**Opening hours**
Mon-Sun
9am-4pm

REUSABLES ACCEPTED   WIFI   BIKE FRIENDLY   DOGS WELCOME   BUY BEANS IN STORE   COFFEE COURSES   OUTDOOR SEATING   CYMRAEG

# 42 96 DEGREES COFFEE

Willow Walk, Old Masons Yard, Cowbridge, Vale of Glamorgan, CF71 7EE

96degreescoffee.co.uk | 01446 774010

f 96degreescoffee @ 96_degreescoffee

**B**aristas are famed for being particular about coffee prep (dialing in each morning, grinding on demand and selecting the best organic milks to complement), but 96 Degrees owner Lee Davies took his penchant for perfection even further when he installed a Giesen roaster in his cafe so he could have total control over the final product.

It's not just Lee who benefits from the investment: as well as an elevated coffee-drinking experience, visitors get to watch the sky-blue roaster in action. Lee roasts during opening hours so patrons can see the process for themselves and ask questions about the coffee's journey from farm to cup.

## TIP PICK UP A BAG OF 96 DEGREES BEANS FROM THE RETAIL SECTION

The cafe's table-service set-up further encourages conversation between coffee drinkers and the 96 Degrees team who are well versed in speciality expertise and pleased to recommend the perfect pour.

All the cakes and traybakes are rustled up in-house and the crew can even craft a bespoke bake for your next celebration.

**Established**
2019

**Key roaster**
96 Degrees Coffee

**Brewing method**
Espresso, V60, batch filter, cold brew

**Machine**
Victoria Arduino Black Eagle

**Grinder**
Mahlkonig EK43, Mahlkonig E65S, Victoria Arduino Mythos One

**Opening hours**
Mon–Fri
8.30am–4pm
Sat
9am–4.30pm
Sun
9.30am–2.30pm

**REUSABLES ACCEPTED**

**WIFI**

**BIKE FRIENDLY**

**BUY BEANS IN STORE**

**OUTDOOR SEATING**

**CYMRAEG**

COWBRIDGE

83

# 43 THE COFFI BOX

Cold Knap Beach, Barry, Vale of Glamorgan, CF62 6TA

**f** *The Coffi Box*  📷 *the_coffi_box*

When Zoey Bailey took on the horsebox that would become her business it was little more than a rusty frame. However, after a lot of love – and some heavy lifting from husband Rich – the rickety structure was transformed into a chic mobile coffee shop.

From Wednesday to Sunday, you'll find the pimped-up horsebox at Cold Knap Beach in Barry. Zoey and the small Coffi Box crew trained with the pros at Hard Lines (who supply their house blend and monthly guest coffee) so are dab hands at pulling silky espresso and dishing out delish filter (available in winter).

## TIP PICK UP A TREAT TO EAT ON THE PEBBLE BEACH – THE COOKIE SLICE IS A GOOD CALL

As the owner of a small business, Zoey is eager to support other indie set-ups. Alongside the Cardiff-roasted coffee, on the drinks list you'll find Flawsome juices (another South Wales biz, this time making delicious drinks from wonky fruit) and Blendsmiths' selection of superfood blends and silky hot chocolates.

She's also serious about sustainability, so The Coffi Box is strictly plastic-free and all packaging is 100 per cent compostable. Take it a step further by rocking up with your reusable cup.

**Established**
2022

**Key roaster**
Hard Lines

**Brewing method**
Espresso,
batch filter

**Machine**
Fracino

**Grinder**
Eureka Helios 80

**Opening hours**
Wed–Sun
10am–4pm

**REUSABLES ACCEPTED**

**BIKE FRIENDLY**

**DOGS WELCOME**

**BUY BEANS IN STORE**

# 44 STOL COFFEE

Penarth, Vale of Glamorgan, CF64 3AU

stolcoffee.co.uk | 07477 114009

f *stolcoffee*  @ *stol_coffee*

This sunshine-yellow coffee cart was rolled out in lockdown to help combat loneliness and bring the people of Penarth together.

During the spring of 2020, barista Piotr Skoczylas wanted to feel closer to his community. To fulfil his aim, he quit his job, invested savings in coffee equipment and a cargo bike, and each morning cycled to the seafront to dish out filter coffee, serve home-baked cookies and start meaningful conversations with his neighbours. The project, which he called Stol, was such a smile-inducing success that it's continued ever since.

## TIP PIOTR WON COVID-19 UNSUNG HERO AT THE THIS CAN HAPPEN AWARDS 2021

You'll find Piotr parked up on Penarth Esplanade from daybreak throughout the week (excluding Mondays) and at Alexandra Park on Sundays. The filter coffee on offer is roasted by Round Hill in Somerset or London's Square Mile, and can be sipped black or with a splash of oat milk.

Seeing as this caffeinated experience is all about good vibes, it would be amiss not to pair your coffee with one of Piotr's pick-me-up vegan brownies or cookies.

**Established**
2020

**Key roaster**
Multiple roasteries

**Brewing method**
Batch filter

**Machine**
Marco BRUF60

**Grinder**
Mahlkonig EK43

**Opening hours**
Tue–Sat
(Penarth Esplanade)
Sunrise
Sun
(Alexandra Park, Penarth)
10am–2pm

**BIKE FRIENDLY**

**DOGS WELCOME**

**BUY BEANS IN STORE**

# 45 QUANTUM COFFEE ROASTERS

58 Bute Street, Cardiff, CF10 5BN
quantumroasters.co.uk | 07413 543335
**f** *quantumroasters* ⭕ *quantumroasters*

When you're ready to branch out from the familiar comfort of house blends and experience the flavour fireworks of single origins, make a beeline for this coffee shop on Cardiff Bay.

Sourcing beans from its own roastery in the city, Quantum specialises in uber rare coffees, most of which are sourced from female producers. This is a place to step out of your comfort zone and challenge your palate.

## TIP CUTTING BACK ON CAFFEINE? TRY THE WATER-PROCESSED CHOCOLATEY DECAF

Typically, two new coffees are introduced each month and launched with a limited-edition spot on the brew bar. Customers are encouraged to sample the fresh single-origins and unique blends via the slow-but-sure means of the V60, which the baristas find best expresses the beans' nuanced flavours.

As well as gaining a following for its constantly evolving catalogue of coffees, Quantum has made a name for itself as a destination for summer refreshment thanks to its nitro cold-brew tap. And, to balance out the seasonal offering across the year, the team have also recently launched a line of luxe Quantum hot chocolates.

**Established**
2015

**Key roaster**
Quantum Coffee
Roasters

**Brewing method**
Espresso, V60,
nitro, cold brew

**Machine**
La Marzocco Linea

**Grinder**
Eureka Drogheria,
Quamar × 2, Zara

**Opening hours**
Mon-Fri
8am-5pm
Sat
9am-5pm
Sun
10am-5pm
(seasonal opening hours)

REUSABLES ACCEPTED   WIFI   BUY BEANS IN STORE   COFFEE COURSES

# 46 THE TRAINING GROUND PROJECT

Grangetown Hub & Library, Havelock Place, Grangetown, Cardiff, CF11 6PA

bossandbrewacademy.co.uk | 07432 533810

ttg.coffee

**C**offee shops are an integral part of local communities, but this cafe within Grangetown Hub takes its role a step further. It's run by a coffee committee made up of young people from the local area who contribute ideas and skills in order to continuously improve the space.

The social enterprise employs recent graduates from Boss & Brew Academy, a not-for-profit that provides free SCA-accredited barista training for young people facing barriers to employment. Behind the bar you'll also find recent school-leavers, who are considering a career in coffee, doing work experience.

## TIP THE BARISTAS LOVE TO SHOW OFF THEIR LATTE ART SKILLS, SO SNAP A PIC AND TAG THEM ON SOCIAL

The baristas may be baby-faced, but don't let that fool you: the coffee served here is some of the best in the area. Beans are sourced from roasteries that create a social impact in their field, such as Manumit, Clifton, Skylark and Redemption, and are prepared as espresso and an array of filter methods.

Before you order, browse the eclectic line-up of cups which have been collected from charity shops around the world. Regulars request their faves, which include cups from as far away as Morocco and China.

**Established**
2022

**Key roaster**
Multiple roasteries

**Brewing method**
Espresso, V60, batch filter, cafetiere, Clever Dripper

**Machine**
La Marzocco Linea PB

**Grinder**
Mahlkonig E65S GbW

**Opening hours**
Mon–Sat
10am–3pm

REUSABLES ACCEPTED    WIFI    BIKE FRIENDLY

# 47 UNCOMMON GROUND COFFEE ROASTERY

10-12 Royal Arcade, Cardiff, CF10 1AE

uncommon-ground.co.uk | 07495 504014

f uncommongroundcoffeeroastery @ _uncommonground

Nestled deep inside Cardiff's historic Royal Arcade, Uncommon Ground's flagship cafe has fuelled local coffee lovers since 2015. One of the area's only roastery-cafes, its popularity is particularly evident on weekend mornings – head there early if you want to sit in.

Once you've snagged a comfy sofa or window seat and you're enveloped in the low-level lighting and industrial-inspired interior, you could be whiling away the hours in a Brooklyn bar, not a Cardiff coffee shop.

## TIP WOKEN UP RAVENOUS? ORDER THE FAMOUS BREAKFAST BURRITO - YOU WON'T BE DISAPPOINTED

Naturally, the coffee in your cup is roasted by the hosts. The Uncommon house espresso is a medium-roast blend of South American and Sumatran beans, so expect plenty of chocolate orange, toffee and plum notes. The filter menu offers single-origin roasts from Central America, East Africa and more.

The counter is always flush with fresh pastries and bakes, but if you're after something more substantial there's also a brunch and lunch menu which features plenty of meat and dairy-free options. The smashed avo on local sourdough is perennially popular.

**Established**
2015

**Key roaster**
Uncommon Ground

**Brewing method**
Espresso, V60, batch filter, cold brew

**Machine**
La Marzocco Linea PB

**Grinder**
Anfim E80

**Opening hours**
Mon-Fri
8.30am-5pm
Sat
9am-5pm
Sun
10am-5pm

**REUSABLES ACCEPTED**

**WIFI**

**DOGS WELCOME**

**BUY BEANS IN STORE**

**COFFEE COURSES**

**OUTDOOR SEATING**

# 48 HARD LINES

Ground Floor, St Canna Court, Cowbridge Road East, Cardiff, CF5 1GX
hard-lines.co.uk
*f hardlinescoffee* *⊚ hardlinescoffee*

Over the past four years, the Hard Lines gang have earned a following for their top-notch coffee and tongue-in-cheek brand. Their beans, packaged in brightly coloured bags adorned with creative illustrations, can be found at speciality coffee shops across the UK, but for the OG Hard Lines experience it's worth making a pilgrimage to the roastery's cafe in Canton.

Inspired by the classic Valleys-Italian cafe experience, the venue on Cowbridge Road East bucks the trend of ultra-minimalist coffee spaces. Diner-style seating, old-school sugar shakers and burritos served in red plastic baskets offer a refreshing contrast to ubiquitous Scandi-chic styling.

## TIP STAYING CENTRAL? PAY A VISIT TO THE SISTER SHOP IN CARDIFF MARKET

At the bar, the team serve two espressos (a classic house roast that tastes great with milk, and a seasonal number that's fun and a little different) and a batch-brew filter, which they recommend pairing with the Hard Lines cult pancake stack. Book a table at the weekend (it gets pretty busy) to chow down on one of their legendary breakfasts.

**Established**
2019

**Key roaster**
Hard Lines

**Brewing method**
Espresso, batch filter, cold brew

**Machine**
La Marzocco KB90

**Grinder**
Mahlkonig EK43,
Mahlkonig E65S × 2

**Opening hours**
Mon-Fri
7.30am–5pm
Sat
8.30am–5pm
Sun
9am–4pm
(seasonal opening hours)

REUSABLES ACCEPTED   WIFI   BIKE FRIENDLY   DOGS WELCOME   BUY BEANS IN STORE   OUTDOOR SEATING   CYMRAEG

# 49 CANNADELI

Unit 2 Pontcanna Mews, 200 Kings Road, Cardiff, CF11 9DF

cannadeli.co.uk | 07973 430596

**f** *cannadeliofficial* **◎** *cannadeli*

Tucked away in a courtyard of indies off Kings Road, this cafe, deli and events space is a hidden haven of great coffee, good food and community connection.

At the start of 2023, former manager Tomos Roberts took over the business and was quick to make his own mark. Improvements included a refresh of the interior to give it a more youthful vibe, a new food menu of brunch and lunch dishes, and a covered and heated outside area which has doubled the venue's capacity.

The house coffee is roasted at the foot of Yr Wyddfa in North Wales by Steffan Huws and the team at Poblado Coffi. It's served as espresso as standard and a wide range of the roastery's beans are sold in retail bags in the deli.

## TIP THE MENU IS ALSO PRINTED IN CYMRAEG AND ALL THE BARISTAS ARE NATIVE SPEAKERS

Trad Welsh dishes such as cawl and rarebit share a menu with crowd-pleasing brunch favourites like jammy eggs with smashed avocado and Black Mountain smoked salmon on rye bread. Make a return trip on Friday evening for CannaNights, a late-night bill of street-food-inspired dishes and drinks.

**Established**
2015

**Key roaster**
Poblado Coffi

**Brewing method**
Espresso

**Machine**
Fracino

**Grinder**
Macap

**Opening hours**
Tue–Sat
9am–5pm
Sun
10am–4pm

WIFI | BIKE FRIENDLY | DOGS WELCOME | BUY BEANS IN STORE | OUTDOOR SEATING | CYMRAEG

# 50 MILKWOOD

83 Pontcanna Street, Cardiff, CF11 9HS
milkwoodcardiff.com | 02920 232226
f *milkwoodcdf* ⊙ *milkwoodcdf*

eafy Pontcanna is carving out a niche as the brunch capital of Cardiff and this cafe with restaurant creds (chef owner Tom Furlong has worked at some of the city's top eateries) is one of the best spots in the neighbourhood.

Classic dishes are elevated and influenced by Welsh ingredients, resulting in a brunch menu like no other. Finish a walk through Bute Park with bacon, cockles and laverbread (a traditional Welsh seaweed delicacy) on toast or fuel a day of indie shopping with a buttermilk fried chicken bun topped with sriracha mayo and house pickles.

## TIP AFTERNOON VISIT? ORDER AN ESPRESSO AND A SLICE OF BURNT BASQUE CHEESECAKE

Good food calls for good coffee, and the Milkwood team source beans from the pros at Clifton Coffee just over the Severn. Espresso may be the only option but the baristas know what they're doing, so killer flat whites come as standard. There's also a strong selection of loose-leaf teas from local blender Waterloo.

On Friday and Saturday evenings, Milkwood leans into its restaurant alter ego. Stick around to chow down on celeriac-schnitzel burgers, cuttlefish ragu and lamb-skewer flatbreads.

**Established**
2015

**Key roaster**
Clifton Coffee
Roasters

**Brewing method**
Espresso

**Machine**
La Marzocco
Linea Classic

**Grinder**
Victoria Arduino
Mythos

**Opening hours**
Mon–Fri
8am–4pm
Sat–Sun
9am–4pm
Fri–Sat evenings
5.30pm–9pm

REUSABLES ACCEPTED | WIFI | BIKE FRIENDLY | DOGS WELCOME | OUTDOOR SEATING | CYMRAEG

# 51 RHOSTIO SPECIALITY COFFEE ROASTERS

16c Crwys Road, Cardiff, CF24 4NJ

rhostio.co.uk | 03300 439593

**f** *rhostiocoffee* **⊙** *rhostio_coffee*

Located in the heart of Cardiff's cultural quarter on buzzy Crwys Road, this spacious multifaceted venue is a hit with young professionals, creatives and families who like to mix up their coffee order.

Two espresso and two batch filter options each week keep the offering fresh. Everything is roasted in-house, so the team can adjust their roasting style and volume depending on what's popular in the cafe. Those who choose to drink in will receive a card crammed with info about the beans they're sipping, including where they were sourced, who grew them and what tasting notes to look out for.

## TIP SUN SHINING? HEAD TO THE ROOFTOP TERRACE FOR A UNIQUE VIEW OF CATHAYS

The roasters host regular cupping sessions in the industrial-chic space, giving local coffee fans the chance to expand their palate. Those who rate the beans can sign up to get them delivered to their door via the Rhostio subscription service.

**Established**
2021

**Key roaster**
Rhostio Speciality
Coffee Roasters

**Brewing method**
Espresso, pourover,
V60, AeroPress,
batch filter

**Machine**
Faema E71

**Grinder**
Victoria Arduino
Mythos One

**Opening hours**
Mon–Thu
9am–7pm
Fri–Sat
9am–10pm
Sun
10am–6pm

**REUSABLES ACCEPTED**

**WIFI**

**BIKE FRIENDLY**

**DOGS WELCOME**

**BUY BEANS IN STORE**

**OUTDOOR SEATING**

# 52 BLŴM

Fairoak House, Fairoak Road, Cardiff, CF24 4YA

blwmhome.co.uk

blwm_cardiff

**S**andwiched between Cardiff's bustling university quarter and leafy Lakeside, this coffee shop and lifestyle store is a favourite with students, families and freelancers.

Visit during the week to blast espresso-fuelled emails from one of the window stools, or drop by at the weekend to catch up with friends over coffee and cake. Whatever the reason for your trip, stopping to browse the retail shelves stocked with locally made candles, ceramics and dried-flower arrangements is a must.

## TIP CHECK INSTAGRAM FOR INFO ON POP-UPS AND EVENTS SUCH AS SEASONAL WREATH CLASSES

The coffee is roasted in Wales by the experienced team at Coaltown and skilfully prepared by the Blŵm baristas who've been trained to ensure every espresso, pourover and flat white is expertly executed. For those looking to shake up their order, there are seasonal specials such as the lavender latte and rose hot chocolate.

Since opening in 2022, Blŵm has built a cult following for its doorstop slices of traybake and mega cookies. A new collab with a local catering company has introduced lunchtime sandwiches, wraps and salads to the line-up.

**Established**
2022

**Key roaster**
Coaltown Coffee Roastery

**Brewing method**
Espresso, V60

**Machine**
La Marzocco Linea PB

**Grinder**
Mahlkonig

**Opening hours**
Mon–Fri
8.30am–4.30pm
Sat–Sun
9am–4pm

REUSABLES ACCEPTED

WIFI

BIKE FRIENDLY

DOGS WELCOME

BUY BEANS IN STORE

OUTDOOR SEATING

CYMRAEG

CARDIFF

# 53 ALEX GOOCH

45 Whitchurch Road, Cardiff, CF14 3JP
alexgoochbaker.com | 07963 605925
**f** *alexgoochbaker* **⊙** *alexgoochbaker*

**B**ite into a chunky slice of sourdough or a lacquered pastry in an indie coffee shop in South Wales and there's a good chance it was baked by the team at Alex Gooch. The award-winning bakery supplies some of the best cafes across the region, including its own four venues (two in Cardiff, one in Radyr and another in Monmouth).

This Whitchurch Road outpost is the original and where locals gather to snaffle chocolate and almond croissants, sink well-made espresso and pick up loaves to lug home. Those who want to stick around to gobble the goods will find plenty of seating, but it's worth arriving early on the weekends as the most desirable pastries get snapped up quickly.

## TIP CHECK OUT WHAT'S ON BATCH FROM THE LIKES OF COALTOWN AND SKYLARK

The Gooch baristas, known locally for their slick latte art skills, have teamed up with the roasters at Clifton Coffee in Bristol to create a bespoke espresso for the cafes. The honey-processed Burundi reveals notes of black cherry, nougat and sultana, and pairs excellently with the bakery's berry bostock. Try it black or with oat milk (the cafe is 100 per cent plant-based).

**WIFI**   **DOGS WELCOME**   **BUY BEANS IN STORE**

**Established**
2021

**Key roaster**
Clifton Coffee
Roasters

**Brewing method**
Espresso, batch
filter, cold brew

**Machine**
La Marzocco
Linea PB

**Grinder**
Mahlkonig EK43 S,
Mahlkonig EK80,
Victoria Arduino
Mythos One

**Opening hours**
Mon–Thu
8am–4pm
Fri–Sat
8am–5pm
Sat–Sun
10am–4pm

# 54 YELLOW CHAIR COFFEE

ION Strength and Conditioning Gym, Unit 12 Cheviot Close, Llanishen, Cardiff, CF14 5JA

07923 141119

🖸 *yellowchaircoffee*

**G**ym goers don't have to settle for a vending machine pick-me-up at Cardiff's ION Strength and Conditioning Gym thanks to its new in-house brew bar.

Whether you're after an espresso hit to get your pump on or caffeination to keep you going post-workout, Yellow Chair Coffee delivers. You don't have to be a gym bunny to visit either; it's open to all from 6am, making it particularly popular with local commuters in need of an early fix.

Speciality beans come courtesy of local roastery Hard Lines and are crafted into top-notch espresso drinks via the La Marzocco machine. Owner and head barista Nalani Baker leads the talented pack who serve killer brews alongside good chat and sweet bakes such as rocky road (you earned it).

### TIP NEED TO COOL DOWN AFTER A SWEATY SESH? THE COLD BREW IS A NO-BRAINER

Don't keep your headphones in while you wait for your coffee – this is a gym after all, so a banging playlist is guaranteed.

**Established**
2023

**Key roaster**
Hard Lines

**Brewing method**
Espresso, cold brew

**Machine**
La Marzocco
Linea Classic

**Grinder**
Victoria Arduino
Mythos One

**Opening hours**
Mon–Fri
6am–1pm
Sat
7am–11pm

CARDIFF

REUSABLES
ACCEPTED

WIFI

BIKE
FRIENDLY

BUY BEANS
IN STORE

OUTDOOR
SEATING

# 55 LONGPLAY

Unit 3 Castle Court Shopping Centre, Caerphilly, CF83 1NU
longplaycoffee.co.uk | 07538 980432
f *longplaycoffeeshop* ⊙ *longplaycoffeeshop*

With its impressive view overlooking the ruins of Caerphilly's medieval castle, this is a picturesque place in which to linger over a carefully crafted cup of something caffeinated.

The town's ancient origins belie the bang-up-to-date coffee offering found at LongPlay. With a house roast that's zipped over from James Gourmet in Ross-on-Wye and a monthly line-up of guests (including Welsh faves Big Dog and Hard Lines), this is an independent coffee shop experience that brings big city vibes to a small town setting.

## TIP A FAB RANGE OF LOOSE-LEAF TEAS INCLUDES THE RUSSIAN CAMEL CARAVAN

The food is treated with as much care as the coffee, so if you're stopping for breakfast, all-day brunch or a toastie you're guaranteed something delish. Don't leave without trying the house croffle, a sugar-glazed toasted croissant served with a topping of your choice – shower it in pecans, maple syrup and butter for an indulgent nutty feast.

**Established**
2022

**Key roaster**
James Gourmet Coffee

**Brewing method**
Espresso, V60, batch filter

**Machine**
La Marzocco Linea Classic

**Grinder**
Anfim Pratica

**Opening hours**
Tue–Sat
9am–4pm
Sun
10am–3pm

**REUSABLES ACCEPTED**

**WIFI**

**BIKE FRIENDLY**

**DOGS WELCOME**

**BUY BEANS IN STORE**

**COFFEE COURSES**

**CYMRAEG**

# 56 BIG DOG COFFEE

138 High Street, Blackwood, Caerphilly, NP12 1AH

bigdogcoffeeco.com | 07824 115795

**f** *bigdogcoffeeco* **◎** *big_dog_coffee*

Two years into running their roastery in Ebbw Vale, Huw and Hannah (founders, siblings and roasters) launched this cafe counterpart in Blackwood. In doing so, the pair gave the people of Caerphilly what they'd been missing: a space to gather and enjoy a super-fresh cup of Big Dog Coffee.

## TIP DON'T BE A CREATURE OF HABIT - SWAP YOUR REGULAR FLAT WHITE ORDER FOR A CUBANO

House, guest, filter and decaf options arrive daily from the roastery HQ and are switched up each month depending on what tastes great. While the beans change, Huw, Hannah and the rest of the BDC crew keep the espresso profile consistent – expect the house espresso to be natural and full-bodied, and the guest coffee to be washed and lightly acidic.

While the espresso options are always a good call, the most exciting coffees are saved for pourover and batch. The baristas favour the filter method for their selection of exotic micro-lots, which change regularly to keep customers on their toes.

Alongside the coffee offering, there's an extensive retail section, book exchange and local artwork, as well as regular events, food pop-ups and yoga classes. Naturally, dogs are very welcome and can be pampered with puppuccinos and pup-friendly ice cream.

**Established**
2022

**Key roaster**
Big Dog Coffee

**Brewing method**
Espresso, Chemex, batch filter

**Machine**
Victoria Arduino Eagle One

**Grinder**
Mahlkonig E65, Mahlkonig E80 GbW

**Opening hours**
Mon–Thu
8am–4pm
Fri
8am–5pm
Sat
9am–4pm
Sun
10am–4pm

**WIFI**

**DOGS WELCOME**

**BUY BEANS IN STORE**

**COFFEE COURSES**

# 57 THE ANGEL BAKERY

50-51 Cross Street, Abergavenny, Monmouthshire, NP7 5EU

theangelbakery.com | 01873 736950

f angelbakeryabergavenny @ angelbakeryabergavenny

Head to the charming market town of Abergavenny, known as the 'Gateway to Wales', to bliss out on a heavenly selection of pastries and speciality coffee at The Angel Bakery.

Located on the edge of Bannau Brycheiniog National Park, it's a fave with ramblers in search of delicious fodder to fuel their pursuits, as well as locals picking up morning pastries, flatties and fresh produce from the on-site shop.

## TIP A SECOND PASTRY FOR LATER IS ALWAYS A GOOD IDEA – ESPECIALLY IF IT'S A FRUITY DANISH

Funky filters and crema-rich espressos are crafted with Round Hill or Hard Lines beans and make a fine pairing to any of the bakes that emerge from the ovens each morning. You can guarantee anything you sink your teeth into will be superb as each sugar-dusted pastry, plump brioche and loaf of chewy sourdough is handmade using flour from British mills.

Don't leave without browsing the cheese counter, organic fruit and veg stand, and shelves packed with seasonal goodies.

**Established**
2016

**Key roaster**
Round Hill Roastery

**Brewing method**
Espresso, filter

**Machine**
Victoria Arduino
Athena Leva

**Grinder**
Mahlkonig EK43,
Mazzer Robur E

**Opening hours**
Tue-Thu
9am-4pm
Fri-Sat
8.30am-3.30pm

REUSABLES ACCEPTED    WIFI    BIKE FRIENDLY    DOGS WELCOME    BUY BEANS IN STORE    OUTDOOR SEATING

ABERGAVENNY

# SOUTH WALES ROASTERIES

# 58 WELSH COFFEE CO.

Unit 4 Kingswood Court, Ogmore Road, Ogmore-by-Sea, Vale of Glamorgan, CF35 5BP

welshcoffee.com | 07900 011244

*f welshcoffeeco* *◎ welshcoffeeco*

I t's no coincidence that this eco coffee company is located a stone's skim from the beach. Founder Huw Williams moved the roastery to the seaside town of Ogmore-by-Sea so he could be closer to his local community – and check the surf from his desk.

Sustainability is paramount for Huw, who established Welsh Coffee Co. in 2011 to reflect his passion for outdoor pursuits such as surfing, walking and yoga. To realise this aim, Huw and team power the roastery using solar-generated electricity, and flame-roast beans in the belly of Dragon, their chunky Probat machine.

**Established**
2011

**Roaster make and size**
Probat 12kg

## 'VISIT TO SAMPLE THE AWARD-WINNING COFFEES WHILE WATCHING WAVES LAP AT THE SHORE'

Their catalogue of coffees features three Great Taste award-winners, including two-star Môr and Bendigadig. Both are South American blends that major on chocolate notes with a touch of tropical fruit. The single-origin selection also zones in on the Americas, and features beans from Nicaragua and Colombia.

To further cement WCC's place in the local community, Huw recently opened a coffee shop in Ogmore-by-Sea's new community hall. Visit to sample the award-winning brews while watching waves lap at the shore below.

OGMORE-BY-SEA

OPEN BY INVITE

COFFEE COURSES

BUY BEANS ONLINE

BUY BEANS IN STORE

CYMRAEG

# 59 HARD LINES

Unit 13 Gwaelod y Garth, Cardiff, CF15 8LA

hard-lines.co.uk

*f hardlinescoffee* © *hardlinescoffee*

Coffee, people and creativity are the guiding principles of this South Wales powerhouse. From responsible sourcing to sustainable roasting and establishing a local running club, Hard Lines founders Sophie Smith and Matt Jones put community first – whether that's close to home or at origin – and like to do things a little differently.

Since its launch in 2017, the roastery has rocketed to the upper echelons of speciality society and its coffee can be found in the hoppers of some of the best cafes in the UK and beyond. While Hard Lines has received great praise (including being shortlisted for a Sprudge design award and mentioned by Yotam Ottolenghi in *The Guardian*), the team haven't let success go to their heads and continue to roast coffee everyone can enjoy.

## 'THE TEAM HAVEN'T LET SUCCESS GO TO THEIR HEADS AND ROAST COFFEE EVERYONE CAN ENJOY'

*'We love to showcase the coffees we love to drink, share our knowledge and are always ready to learn,'* says Sophie.

On Fridays, the roastery in the shadow of Castell Coch (just outside Cardiff) opens its doors for takeaway brews, but the roomier cafe space in Canton slings shots and pours juicy batch brew all week long. If you're in the city centre, Hard Lines' stall in Cardiff Market is open for business every day except Sundays.

**Established**
2017

**Roaster make and size**
Loring S15
Falcon 15kg

CAFE ON SITE    OPEN BY INVITE    COFFEE COURSES    BUY BEANS ONLINE    BUY BEANS IN STORE    CYMRAEG

# 60 BIG DOG COFFEE

Unit 20 The Innovation Centre, Festival Drive, Ebbw Vale, Blaenau Gwent, NP23 8XA

bigdogcoffeeco.com | 07824 115795

*f bigdogcoffeeco* *☺ big_dog_coffee*

This Ebbw Vale roastery is going from strength to strength. Since it was launched by siblings Huw and Hannah in 2020, Big Dog has grown to include a speciality cafe in Caerphilly and welcomed five employees into the fold.

While the business has bloomed, the roasting team have kept the BESCA firing with a line-up of interesting beans from across the world. The Big Dog catalogue features blends, single estates and decafs, and there's even a Black Box Coffee range which showcases experimental processes and micro-lots.

## 'ON A MISSION TO MAKE GOOD COFFEE ACCESSIBLE TO ALL'

The team have established direct-trade relationships with farms in Brazil, Timor-Leste and Uganda, and the success of the projects has birthed further plans to work more closely with other farmers at origin.

Producing exceptional beans and building on South Wales' reputation for speciality are priorities for Huw and Hannah. However, they're also on a mission to make good coffee accessible to all – whether they're caffeine enthusiasts or casual cappuccino drinkers. From the packaging and description of each roast to the approachable and friendly demeanour of the team, this is a people-driven roastery.

**Established**
2020

**Roaster make and size**
BESCA 5kg

OPEN TO
THE PUBLIC

COFFEE
COURSES

BUY BEANS
ONLINE

BUY BEANS
IN STORE

# 61 BOSS & BREW ACADEMY

Wales Millennium Centre, Bute Place, Butetown, Cardiff, CF10 5AL

bossandbrewacademy.co.uk | 07432 533810

*f Boss & Brew Academy* 🄾 *bossandbrewacademy*

'**C**offee in one hand, confidence in the other' is the motto of this barista training academy and social enterprise that helps young people facing barriers to employment gain the skills needed to work in the speciality coffee industry.

Located within Cardiff Bay's iconic Wales Millennium Centre, Boss & Brew was established by certified AST trainer Natalie Hodgkinson in 2021 as a space to deliver SCA-accredited courses for the local community. To date she's trained 136 baristas, with many going on to work in cafes in Cardiff and beyond.

**Established**
2021

## 'COFFEE IS THE MEDIUM WE USE TO INSPIRE, UPLIFT AND EMPOWER PEOPLE'

*'We strive to provide a safe space where young people can develop new skills, explore their talents and grow in confidence,'* says Natalie. *'Coffee is simply the medium we use to inspire, uplift and empower people.'*

As well as offering fully funded courses for those in need, Boss & Brew hosts barista experiences for small groups and one-to-one sessions. A Boss & Brew coffee cart is also available to hire for events, providing work experience opportunities for its trainees.

SCA COFFEE
COURSES

COFFEE
COURSES

CYMRAEG

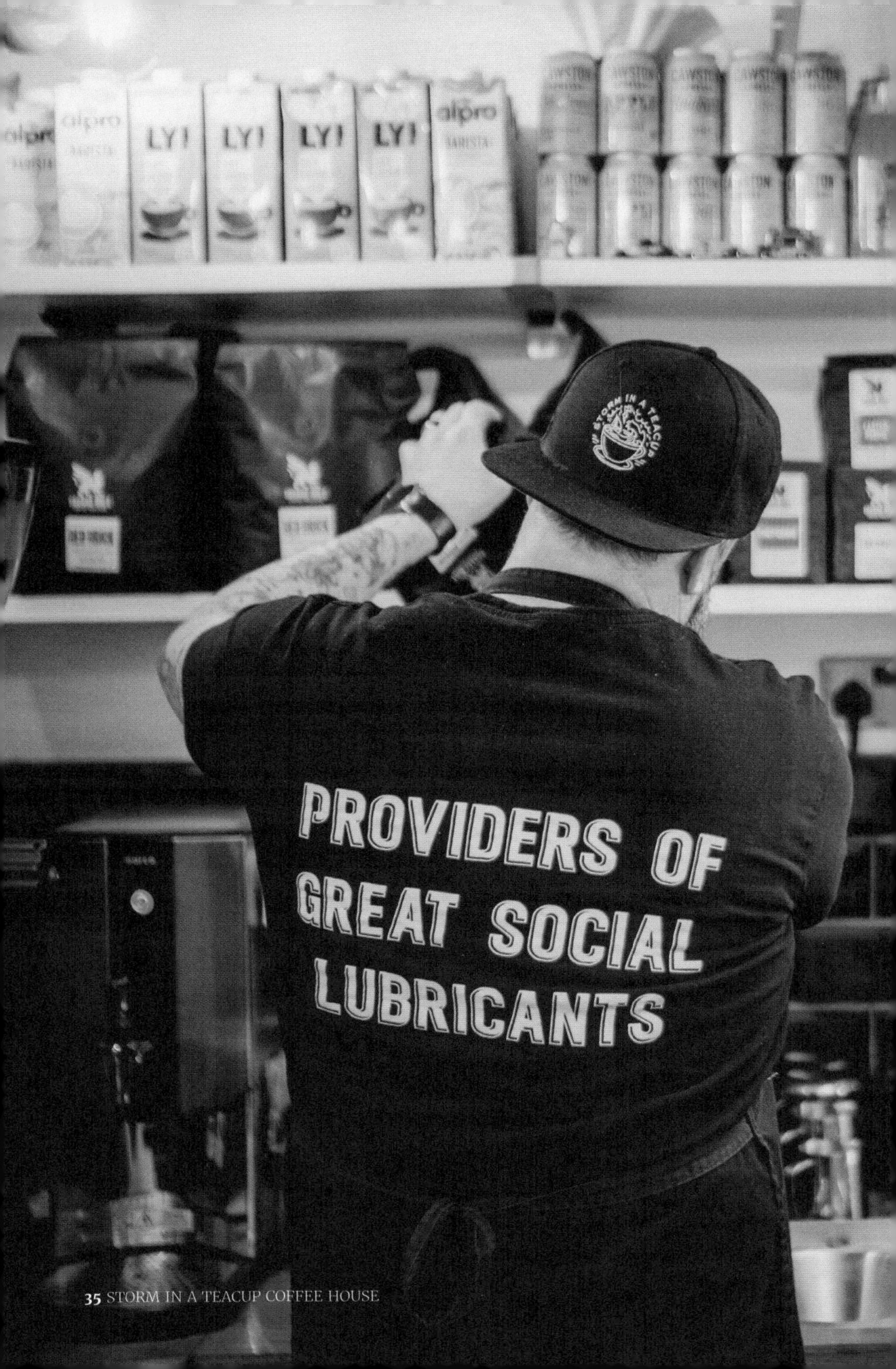
STORM IN A TEACUP
PROVIDERS OF
GREAT SOCIAL
LUBRICANTS

# MORE GOOD
# COFFEE
# SHOPS

## MORE PLACES TO DRINK
## EXCEPTIONAL COFFEE

## 62 BEAN & BREAD
36 Lion Street, Abergavenny,
Monmouthshire, NP7 5PE
**beanandbread.co.uk**

## 63 BOO'S KITCHEN
2 Woodville Road, Mumbles,
Swansea, SA3 4AD

## 64 BRØD - BAKERY & HATCH
Unit 14-15 Riverbridge Business Park,
Cardiff, CF23 9FP
**thedanishbakery.co.uk**

## 65 BRØD - PENARTH
6 Glebe Street, Penarth, Vale of
Glamorgan, CF64 1EB
**thedanishbakery.co.uk**

## 66 BRØD - PONTCANNA
126 Wyndham Crescent, Cardiff, CF11 9EG
**thedanishbakery.co.uk**

## 67 BRODIES BRICKS 'N' MORTAR
56 North Road, Cardiff, CF10 3DZ
**brodiescoffee.co.uk**

## 68 BRODIES COFFEE CABIN
Gorsedd Gardens, Cardiff, CF10 3NP
**brodiescoffee.co.uk**

## 69 CORNER COFFEE
13 High Street, Cardiff, CF10 1AX
**cornercoffee.uk**

## 70 CRWST
Priory Street, Cardigan,
Ceredigion, SA43 1BU
**crwst.cymru**

## 71 KIN + ILK
31 Cathedral Road, Pontcanna,
Cardiff, CF11 9HB
**kinandilk.com**

## 72 MOTLEY PIE & COFFEE
Woodlands Terrace, Gowerton,
Swansea, SA4 3DP
**motleypie.co.uk**

## 73 SIBLING
39 Lochaber Street, Cardiff, CF24 3LS
**siblingcardiff.co.uk**

## 74 SOCIAL EATS
20 Salisbury Road, Cardiff, CF24 4AD

## 75 SPARROW COFFEE HOUSE
146 Clifton Street, Cardiff, CF24 1PU

## 76 THE LITTLE MAN COFFEE CO. - CARDIFF
Ivor House, Bridge Street,
Cardiff, CF10 2EE
**little-man-coffee.myshopify.com**

## 77 THE LITTLE MAN COFFEE CO. - SWANSEA
24 Wind Street, Swansea, SA1 1DY
**little-man-coffee.myshopify.com**

## 78 WATERLOO TEA
41 Wellfield Road, Cardiff, CF24 3PA
**waterlootea.com**

## 79 WELSH COFFEE CO. - COFFEE TRUCK
Ogmore Beach, Ogmore-by-Sea,
Vale of Glamorgan
**welshcoffee.com**

## 80 WRIGHT'S
Llanarthne, Carmarthenshire, SA32 8JU
**wrightsfood.co.uk**

# MORE GOOD
# ROASTERIES

## ADDITIONAL PLACES TO SOURCE BEANS FOR YOUR HOME HOPPER

WELSH COFFEE CO.

## 81 ALFIE'S COFFEE CO.
8 Heol Rhosybonwen, Cefneithin,
Carmarthenshire, SA14 6TF
**alfiescoffeeco.co.uk**

## 82 COFFI ERYRI
Hafod y Geunan, Nebo, Llanrwst,
Conwy, LL26 0TD
**coffieryri.cymru**

## 83 FFA DA
Llandanwg, Gwynedd, LL46 2SD
**ffada.co.uk**

## 84 FOOTPRINT
Ednol Farm, Kinnerton,
Presteigne, Powys, LD8 2PF
**footprintcoffee.co.uk**

## 85 MANUMIT COFFEE ROASTERS
Cardiff
**manumitcoffee.co.uk**

## 86 QUANTUM COFFEE ROASTERS
58 Bute Street, Cardiff, CF10 5BN
**quantumroasters.co.uk**

## 87 UNCOMMON GROUND COFFEE ROASTERY
Pontcynon Industrial Estate, Abercynon,
Mountain Ash, CF45 4EP
**uncommon-ground.co.uk**

## 88 WREXHAM BEAN CO.
35 Chester Street, Wrexham, LL13 8AH
**wrexhambean.com**

# MEET OUR COMMITTEE

The *Indy Coffee Guide Wales* committee is made up of a small band of leading coffee experts from across the country, who work with Salt Media and the coffee community to oversee the creation of this guide

## Scott James

Scott is founder of Coaltown Coffee, a speciality roastery in Ammanford, Carmarthenshire. In 2019, it became the first speciality coffee roastery in the UK to earn B Corp certification, in part thanks to Scott's *'people before profit'* approach.

*'We believe in bringing new industry to post-industrial towns across the UK. We started with our hometown and used coffee, a new "black gold", to fuel it,'* says Scott. *'Sourcing from truly ethical producers and paying people properly make a positive difference at both ends of the supply chain.'*

## Sophie Smith

Sophie started Hard Lines in Cardiff with Matt Jones in 2016. What began as a humble AeroPress bar turned into two bricks-and-mortar sites and their own roastery. The team select, roast and serve speciality coffee that's been sourced sustainably with the aim of building relationships at origin.

*'Hard Lines is a fun, energetic and creative coffee brand,'* says Sophie. *'We challenge ourselves to do things differently and shake things up. Our goal is to build long-lasting relationships with producers and communities around the world.'*

## Steffan Huws

Steffan started Poblado Coffi in 2013, when he invested in a 5kg Toper which he installed in his shed. Over the past decade, his roastery on the edge of Eryri National Park has steadily grown while staying true to its founding mission of being an ethical business.

*'The quality of our produce is of equal importance to the relationships we develop with our customers, suppliers and the producers themselves,'* says Steffan.

# NOTES

Somewhere to keep a record of exceptional
beans and brews you've discovered on your
coffee adventures

# NOTES

Somewhere to keep a record of exceptional
beans and brews you've discovered on your
coffee adventures

# NOTES

Somewhere to keep a record of exceptional
beans and brews you've discovered on your
coffee adventures

# NOTES

Somewhere to keep a record of exceptional beans and brews you've discovered on your coffee adventures

# NOTES

Somewhere to keep a record of exceptional beans and brews you've discovered on your coffee adventures

# FOR BREW FREAKS, BEAN GEEKS